D0856203

JOHN FOWLES,
Magus and Moralist

By the Same Author:

The Disciplined Heart: Iris Murdoch and Her Novels
Dreamers Who Live Their Dreams: The World of Ross
Macdonald's Novels
Graham Greene the Entertainer
Mary Renault
Rebecca West: Artist and Thinker

JOHN FOWLES,
Magus and Moralist

Peter Wolfe

Lewisburg
BUCKNELL UNIVERSITY PRESS
London: Associated University Presses

©1976 by Associated University Presses, Inc.

Associated University Presses, Inc.
Cranbury, New Jersey 08512

Associated University Presses
108 New Bond Street
London W1Y OQX, England

Library of Congress Cataloging in Publication Data
Wolfe, Peter, 1933-
John Fowles, magus and moralist.

Bibliography: p.
Includes index.
1. Fowles, John, 1926- —Criticism and
interpretation. I.   Title.
PR6056.085Z9 1976   823'.9'14   75-5149
ISBN 0-8387-1700-4

Contents

Preface

A rough talley in a publishers' trade journal in 1972 said that John Fowles's three novels, *The Collector* (1963), *The Magus* (1965), and *The French Lieutenant's Woman* (1969), had sold more than four million copies in paperback reprints alone. Since that time, during which the novels have continued to sell both in paperback and hardcover, Fowles has been a frequent subject of articles, book chapters, theses, and dissertations; his work is taught in college classes in both modern and, owing to the Victorian tone and setting of *The French Lieutenant's Woman,* Victorian fiction; though no cult hero, he has won praise from intelligent nonspecialists for giving British fiction an intellectual drive perhaps lacking since Joyce.

How does Fowles present sophisticated ideas without boring or force-feeding the common reader? How has he leveled the barrier between the common reader and literature? No answer comes to mind. Anybody who could supply one in a short paragraph would not have needed to devote a book to the questions. Artistic creation grows more mysterious and more reluctant to release its treasures in direct ratio to the stature of the artist. Though Fowles has worn a path between academe and the marketplace, he also defies us to trace his footsteps.

More practical for us would be to take a short look both

at the man behind the fiction and the commitments that give the fiction its force. John Fowles was born 31 March 1926, at Leigh-on-Sea, Essex, England. He attended Bedford School and then Oxford University (New College) from 1947-50, where he earned honors in French. Between 1944-47, he served as a Lieutenant in the Royal Marines. His main civilian job, until he became a full-time writer, was that of a teacher, first overseas and then at home. He taught, with the rank of Lecteur, at the University of Poitiers in France during the 1950-51 academic year; for the next two years (1951-53), he was on the faculty of Anargyrios College of Spetsai, Greece, later transformed into the Lord Byron School and the Greek island of Phraxos in *The Magus.* He concluded his teaching career with a number of posts in England, 1953-63, all teaching English language and literature to foreigners. The popularity of *The Collector* freed him from working for a salary. Since 1963 he has been writing and living in Dorset, England, with his wife Elizabeth, whom he married in 1956, and their daughter.

Fowles's artistry imitates the divine act of creation in a mirroring universe. His creative job he gladly shares. Like any good novelist, he discovers himself through characters who are discovering and creating themselves amid the raw stuff of every day. It is not his ideas but the skill and verve with which they are conveyed that make him so exciting. Fowles deals with human issues through confrontation, not isolation. These issues include the ancient and important ones of chance (or hazard), evolution, and the need to appreciate the healing, comforting influence of women—the industrial West, he believes, has failed to temper the male virtues of bravery, ambition, and endurance with female benevolence and gentleness. The imbalance between male and female principles has had damaging reverberations; besides blocking the interchange and freedom necessary to the formation of a civilization, it also thwarts mankind's best hope: evolution.

Fowles's attitude toward and treatment of his leading themes reveal a heart for wholeness. No grudges, pity, or special pleading cloud his art. Shored up by a healthy inclusiveness, he is one of today's most cheerful, welcoming novelists. Perhaps no male writer in English since Keats has been so comfortable with the accidental and contingent. His characters have wills and hearts, private histories and individual speaking styles. He believes in the dynamism of ideas. Yet he has an unusual tenderness for insects and greenery; a regular reviewer of nature books for the *New Statesman,* he has also published essays on ecology and conservation (symbolizing the moral bleakness of his title character in *The Collector* is a collection of dead butterflies).

What will happen to his vision is an open question. Art selects; by describing a selected event and then trying to discover its meaning, it also gives form to life. Braced by his studies in Zen, Fowles may be nearing the point where meaning and enactment fuse. If this happens, his commitment to life will express itself privately. He will have outgrown his need to write. Perhaps his small output of books indicates this auctorial silence as his aim; a major character in *The Magus* says that there are times when silence is a poem. Meanwhile, his hold on life is firm, his vision steady, and his vocation secure. His insistence that we evolve through hazard rather than through ready-made ideologies or material ownership challenges us all to be a little more human.

The time and energy of a number of people went into the preparation of this book. Special thanks are owed to Charles Dougherty and James Tierney for their kind help with organization and style, to Audria Shumard for typing the manuscript, and to the University of Missouri-Saint Louis for grants to cover expenses connected with the manuscript's preparation.

The combined help of the following people amounts to a major contribution: Geoffrey Gosling, Barbara Shreckengost, Marcus Allen, Michael Rowland, Mara Ervi Masellis, Mary Finn, Ginni Bowie, Patrick Perrone, Victoria Bush, and Oran Plaisir.

Acknowledgments

The author and publisher join in expressing their thanks for permission to quote copyrighted passages to the following: from *The Collector, The Aristos, The Magus,* and *The French Lieutenant's Woman,* by permission of Little, Brown and Company, and by permission of Anthony Sheil Associates Limited and Jonathan Cape, Inc.; from *Counterpoint* by Roy Newquist, copyright 1964 by Rand McNally & Company; from T.S. Eliot's "Little Gidding," by permission of Harcourt Brace Jovanovich.

1
The Passion to Exist

John Fowles is a literary artist. He ponders serious ideas, he probes the recesses of personality, and he writes in a style that can do anything he asks of it. What makes him so vital to our needs, apart from the challenges he rises to, is his rootedness in everyday experience. Fowles's faith in life goes a long way. Reality is hugely alive for him; with the self-detachment of an Eastern mystic, he wants only to be on a level with it. To constitute life is both to celebrate and create it. Refusing to back away from people, his work has an inclusiveness rare in today's fiction. He is a novelist of being. His characters usually live in ordinary houses on ordinary streets; they hold jobs; in their spare time, they drink in pubs and fall in love.

This ordinary world he heightens, interprets, and bathes in the glow of intellectual and social history. What he does not do is to reduce his commitment to formula or abstraction. Instead, he improvises commitment. His novels are written at a high level of physical perception. They transmit sight and sound, meaning and texture, all at once. No character is posed; no idea flattened to direct statement. All are caught on the wing, at the moment of vivid life and mobility. Pledged to individual freedom, Fowles does not replace characterization by a sociology of distinctions. Each person is an independent center of significance. Nobody exists to serve the state or to flesh out a relationship. To label a person or to define him instrumentally both dwarfs him and clouds one's own perception.

Fowles's combination of enthusiasm, erudition, and human insight makes for a stunning achievement. His novels are brilliant performances, and Fowles has even described himself as a showman-performer: "In my novels I am the producer, director, and all the actors; I photograph it . . . . There *is* a vanity about it, a wish to play the godgame." [1] And in *The French Lieutenant's Woman,* where he impishly appears twice, he has "a distinct touch of the flashy. He looks very much as if he has given up preaching and gone in for grand opera . . . . There is, in short, more than a touch of the successful impresario about him." The tension playfully alluded to here between preaching, or instruction, and grand opera, or entertainment, energizes all his novels. If an imbalance between the counterforces exists, then the showman is crowding out the teacher, as the quotation suggests. (Perhaps Fowles's acceptance of a free, systemless reality will occur when the showman takes over completely; or, to suggest a total acceptance, when Fowles stops writing.) *The Collector* (1963) turns on Fowles's masterstroke of using two people who have nothing to say *to* and no use *for* each other and of building out of their nonrelationship a metaphysical drama for our time. The firework display in *The Magus* (1965) shows illusion and reality both changing places and interpenetrating. The world of *The French Lieutenant's Woman* (1969) is both larger and more precise than those of its forerunners. A master entertainer, Fowles puts on a great show in his magical mystery tour through Victorian England. He knows Victorian politics and clothing styles, religious trends and interior decorating. He treats the reader to pocket histories of farm labor and contraception. In a footnote, he analyzes a Tennyson lyric. He goes into a great London department store, introduces the store's personnel, and shows its wares.

The reader becomes acquainted with a doctor, a lawyer, a minister, a London streetwalker, and various servants. Out of the city, one visits a country estate, a rural Dorsetshire village, and a seaside vacation resort.

This brilliant panorama goes beyond showmanship. Though Fowles stands at the center of his work, he makes himself invisible. His characters have appetites and wills, and they generate serious effects. Through them, he teaches, touches our hearts, and says something about humanity. In a 1965 interview, he distinguished between art and entertainment. Art takes a philosophical and moral stand. It avoids cliquishness, surface dazzle, and a preoccupation with technique:

> All good books are distilled experience . . . . I think the serious writer has to have his view of the purpose of literature absolutely clear. I don't see that you can write seriously without having a philosophy of both life and literature to back you. Some philosophy of life is a property of all better writers. [2]

Fowles's invisibility supports his claim that the individual is the seat of all value. Like D.H. Lawrence, Fowles wants to raise the quality, not the standard, of living. This improvement he sees in private terms, not social or political ones. Though he does not believe in absolute human freedom, his agenda for reform both starts and ends with the self. Parliamentary or Supreme Court decisions do not touch people as deeply as their own personal resolves. They have to make up their minds and then take charge of themselves.

The preservation of individual freedom is a philosophical issue that glows more brightly in French than in English literature. So whereas Fowles writes about English themes, he buttresses them with French tough-mindedness and intellectual stamina: "The French school of novelists," which includes Sartre and Simone de Beauvoir, has a "serious view of the writer's function" he shares "absolutely": "I feel I must be committed, that I must use literature as a method of propagating my view of life." Writing about the literature of extreme situations, which stresses the primacy of individual choice, he says, "I would like to see more of this serious and didactic approach."[3] Though contingent, we can still make sense of our lives. Life is not hostile. Rather than preparing us for a leap, Fowles helps us cope. The stripping away of personality and the existential leap only come after all is lost. Fowles's love of the commonplace precludes this desperation. People are both permeated and surrounded by rich, close-crowding life. Fowles refuses to sacrifice this density to a code or creed. Like any good philosopher, he does not let what we might be weaken what we are. Joyce Carol Oates hit the proper descriptive note for him in 1969 when she called him "half scholar and half magus."[4]

I

Most of Fowles's polemic comes in a work called *The Aristos* (1964; revised edition, 1970). Subtitled *A Self-portrait in Ideas,* Fowles's only nonfictional book has gained little favor. Even his own attitude toward the book is mixed. Although "a lot of it was completely misfired flamboyance," he nevertheless considers *The Aristos* "a mistake he would go on making."[5] Robert Scholes describes it as "a collection of philosophical workpoints"; Marvin Mudrick, lacing his wit with sarcasm, calls it "sawdust from Nietzsche's lumber room."[6] The implied parallel with *Thus Spoke Zarathustra* has merit. Like Nietzsche's work, *The Aristos* is aphoristic and teleological; it also views social- and self-transcendence as distant, but worthwhile, goals. *The Aristos* is not so much prophecy, philosophy, or political science as the raw stuff of these endeavors. Yet its patchwork of ideas knits as both attitude and argument. It puts forward a few principles, shows where man has gone wrong, and gives some advice on how the wrongs can be set right. It is, in short, a witty, crotchety book founded on man's potential to know, save, and overcome himself.

The books's crotchets do not rankle. Although ambitious in scope, *The Aristos* states its case modestly, issues no plea, and makes no claims. Fowles's terming it merely one side of a dialogue invites the reader to ignore or reject as he pleases. Further, by making his judgments tentative, Fowles also reserves the right to change his own mind. The differences between the 1964 and 1970 editions of the book, though, are more illustrative than thematic. He may update an argument in the light of a public event that occurred between 1964-70, like Robert Kennedy's death; but beyond bringing in new evidence, he adds little. Where the editions differ is in their approach and method. For the sake of clarity and emphasis, the later one rearranges some of the chapters or groups of notes. Clarity and emphasis also prompt Fowles to shift a note, or entry, or sometimes even a whole subgroup of notes, from one chapter to another. The greatest changes come in the excisions; the cutting out of certain passages changes the tone of the book more than the addition of others. The 1970 revision of *The Aristos* runs about ten percent shorter than the original. It has more force because it is less digressive, self-indulgent, and coy. Fowles himself complained in his introduction that the 1964 text was marred by "an irritating swarm of new-coined words," like Agora society, Stoa society, and Parahades. These neologisms he deletes from the revision, along with personal anecdotes and witty irreverences like, "If Jesus came to Rome tomorrow, he would catch the next plane to Peking." Although both versions of *The Aristos* qualify as intellectual self-portraits, the added maturity, balance, and topicality of the revision give the 1970 text a greater urgency and relevance.

Both versions, though, present their data in the same way—as notes. Fowles arranges these notes in thematic groups ("The Tensional Nature of Human Reality," "The Obsession with Money," and so forth). But beyond organizing his data, he does not impose his will or personality on them. No consecutive argument runs though *The Aristos.* Nor does Fowles use style as a persuader. He will speak in metaphor or symbol, but only to clarify; not to heighten or dazzle. "To banish all possibility of persuasion by artificial means" is to give his ideas an independent life. By deliberately suppressing rhetoric, he forces his ideas to stand on their own. Whatever acceptance they gain must come from their merit rather than from being "likeably presented" by the notable author of *The Collector* and *The Magus.*

The range of voices in *The Aristos* deserves comment. Fowles sees life through the eyes of a literary artist. He can be matter-of-fact, cryptic, rhapsodic, urbane, or analytical. Some of his insights are poetic and revelatory; others, backed by statistics, are cognitive and scientific. The Mayfair wag becomes the analyst or parable teller without warning. Subject matter determines style. For instance, the first group of notes uses the metaphor of the raft to describe human contingency: We are drifting somewhere between two golden ages but without a paddle or motor to take us to either one. The metaphor makes the twofold point that being has intrinsic merit and that traveling hopefully toward a goal surpasses arriving. Elsewhere, Fowles will use symbols, epigrams, or aphorisms to move closer to his subject. This practice of going beyond consecutive discourse carries into his novels. Both philosophically and rhetorically, *The Aristos* fits with Fowles's other work. Its hyperboles look ahead to Charles Smithson's first private extended view of the title character of *The French*

Lieutenant's Woman, in which "the whole Victorian Age was lost." Accordingly, the paradox that brightens *The Aristos* flickers just as vividly elsewhere. A character in *The Magus* is called "eternally the victor in a war where the losers win," and Thomas Hardy comes to us as "a kind of giant mouse"[7] in a 1970 book review.

This rich figurative language captures some of the complexity of life. Fowles, as has been stated, finds mystery and excitement in daily living. This complex, omniform reality can not be compassed by any one rhetorical mode. Human uniqueness, the creative artist's stock and trade, shatters the bounds set by rational discourse. Reason's avoidance of mystery and emotion denies rational discourse access into the imagination. Man cannot be framed by a theory or an arbitrary construct like language. But where do the limits of language leave Fowles? A writer, he cannot escape using words. What he does bypass is the reductiveness and manipulative jargon imposed by a single voice or vocabulary. *The Aristos* uses many rhetorical modes; *The Collector* employs alternating diaries and antiphonal voices to convey moral distinctions; the polystylism of *The Magus* lowers barriers between reader and character and also between life and art; the Victorian manner of *The French Lieutenant's Woman* helps develop important ties between our century and the nineteenth. As shall be seen, Fowles views art as the best kind of human communication; literature, because of the subtlety and inclusiveness of language, he views as the premier art form.

But literature has only instrumental value. Life always comes first and Fowles's commitment to it needs no heightening, either in literature or metaphysics. Instead of searching out theoretical sanctions, he brings history to a living stop—the now. God certifies His existence by not governing the universe in any observable way: "If there had been a creator, his second act would have been to disappear" (*The Aristos*); "I ask God never to reveal himself to me. Because if he did I should know that he was not God. But a liar" (*The Magus*); "There is only one good definition of God: the freedom that allows other freedoms to exist" (*The French Lieutenant's Woman*). In the divine realm, absence does not denote nonbeing; absence is, in fact, a diving attribute. God is not an activity or force; He is a context in which activity occurs, a dimension that houses and nourishes other dimensions. Conscious and partisan, He sympathizes with the whole, the macrocosm, rather than with the individual. But He never sacrifices the part to the whole gratuitously or cruelly. Though the universe does not seem organized to make us happy, it does befriend our long-range needs: "If the individual thing suffers, it is so that the whole may not" (*The Aristos*). If the death of a few prolongs the whole and thereby allows many to thrive, then the world has gained a bargain. So even though the individual is ruled by chance, the whole works by fixed law. But this law exerts itself inscrutably. One only knows of its existence because it obeys the principle that any creator must appear free of its creation: any creation that reveals its internal machinery forfeits spontaneity and self-determination. By staying hidden, God forces us to make our own way. Even an orthodox believer must disregard God sometimes. Otherwise, he could not learn the self-control and responsibility to fend for himself. Free will is a function of human contingency; unless we act and fight alone, we lose the chance to take charge of our lives.

Belief in an afterlife also betrays individual freedom. Like the concept of a soul, to which it is usually linked, it undermines the now. Its refusal to see life as terminal and absolute keeps one from being adult. What is worse, it encourages moral escapism, divides one from reality, and subordinates human injustice to the dangerous myth of a just eternity. To Fowles, all human values flow from lived experience: "Convince a man that he has only this life," he says in *The Aristos,* "and he will do what most of us do about the houses we live in."

Life thus becomes its own object. Our dogmas take on only instrumental or situational value. They exist as means, helping us live and feel what we believe. Rather than constituting life, they give life form and strengthen our decisions about it: they help us make the best of what we have and what we are. The philosophy best able to equip man for survival is that of existentialism. Now existentialism, as Fowles terms it, is not a system of creeds and caveats. Doctrineless, it is a tool or utility. It selects from other philosophies to help cope with a given situation. Fowles praised existentialism to Roy Newquist in 1965:

> This giving of a solution is the wonderful thing about existentialism . . . . It allows you to face reality and act creatively in terms of your own powers and your own situation. It's the great individualist philosophy, the twentieth-century individual's answer to the evil pressures of both capitalism and communism.[8]

Existentialism does not try to detach people from their moral and social backgrounds. Instead, it holds the proper balance between the individual and his tradition. This balance keeps shifting because each new situation calls for a reassessment of motives and needs within a changing context. Only after this reassessment of variables takes place does the existentialist choose.

Existentialism's commitment to positive action also counts heavily for Fowles. Existentialism is an action philosophy. Discouraging passive thought, it favors direct participation. The existentialist discovers reality by acting on it. Goodness means enactment. It is not enough to admire or want the good. To solve the anxieties and frustrations of life, man has to join the skirmish, even if skirmishing is dangerous. Truth comes only in terror and loss, not in doctrine or fact. It grips one's whole person. There is a private, nameless kernel of selfhood in all of us that cannot be escaped or broken down. This central knot of self, that is, individuality, makes individual decisions.

Important acts are always unique. Collectivism downgrades the faculties freedom prizes most—individual reason and choice. Fowles says in *The Aristos,* "Man should not be, above all, necessary to society; he should be above all necessary to himself." Maurice Conchis, his spokesman in *The Magus,* claims, "The most important questions in life can never be answered by anyone except oneself." Conchis's dictum is borne out by Nicholas Urfe, the book's main character and narrator. Most of the key events in Urfe's life happen when he is alone; most of his key decisions are forced on him by chance. His separation anxiety makes him representative. Like him, Frederick Clegg of *The Collector* and the three main characters of *The French Lieutenant's Woman* are only children whose loneliness deepens as they grow older. They all view themselves as outcasts, and all must face their ordeals alone. Clegg, Urfe, and Charles Smithson have no parents. Alison Kelly, Urfe's sweetheart, says, "I just have people I like. Or love. They're the only homeland I have left." Since her love-relationships bring her pain and guilt, she often finds herself as homeless and lonely as Frederick Clegg in his collecting obsession.

Now whereas all knowledge comes from self-knowledge, the goal of both freedom and self-knowledge is integration. Man is a social creature, and so long as he detaches himself from other people his perceptions run to waste. However urgent our revelations, they need sharing. They have to prepare us for commitment to something outside ourselves. *The Aristos* claims that most organizations, fearing imagination and free will, break on the rock of individuality. Yet elsewhere the book says that social conformity is sometimes useful and worthwhile. The creed of self, for all its color, can lead to anarchy. Its refusal to detach conduct from self-interest encourages the most hidebound creed of all, unrestricted free enterprise. Freedom is by nature competitive. Since anybody's freedom must respect everybody else's, the pull between conflicting freedoms must be regulated. Fowles recognizes this need by using Matthew Arnold's warning of the dangers of unbridled freedom as an epigraph to one of the chapters in *The French Lieutenant's Woman:*

> More and more this and that man, and this and that body of men, all over the country, are beginning to assert and put in practice an Englishman's right to do what he likes; his right to march where he likes, meet where he likes, enter where he likes, hoot as he likes, threaten as he likes, smash as he likes. All this, I say, tends to anarchy.
>
> Matthew Arnold Culture and Anarchy (1869)

While close to Arnold's, Fowles's view of freedom is more revisionist. Freedom for Fowles has no absolute value. Like any other blind force, it is amoral, colorless, neither good nor bad. Since goodness and freedom are not synonymous, free acts do not always promote virtue and goodness. Gratuitous acts, for instance, only show contempt for convention. Sexual freedom, too, is full of dangers. The evils of free love go beyond sexual promiscuity to produce a social cancer. "Free love does not encourage true love," argues Fowles in *The Aristos:*

> The emotional instability that gets one into bed is unlikely to change into the emotional stability one needs when one has to get out. Venereal diseases spread. Neuroses spread. Broken marriages increase, and the innocent children of them suffer, and in their turn breed suffering.

If the gratuitous act and promiscuous sex both pervert freedom, freedom sometimes affirms itself negatively, that is, by refraining from positive action: any definition of freedom includes the right *not* to act. The benefits reaped by cowardice prove that deliberate inaction can work in life's favor. Foresight keeps us from taking foolish risks and thus preserves us. Because of this brake, our acts do not betray us as do those of animals, who cannot foresee consequences.

Fowles's argument gives comfort, proving that freedom has real value. What it does not ascertain is freedom's scope. But he cannot be blamed. We lack the evolutionary and biological information to know whether we possess free will. All we can say is that what passes for freedom with us is not total: "To be completely free we should need an absolutely free field of choice as well as the freedom to choose in it" (*The Aristos*). We are in fact hemmed in by realities beyond our control—our sex, our parentage, the environment in which we were born. Freedom exists, at best, relatively. Fowles uses the metaphor of the prison to express this relativism: "We are in a prison cell, but it is, or can be made to become, a comparatively spacious one; and inside it we can become relatively free" (*The Aristos*). In *The Magus,* the metaphor of the zoo replaces that of the prison: the "subtle psychosexual bars" holding Nicholas Urfe inside the Godgame leave him a wide berth: "If you have a private menagerie, your concern is to keep the animals in, not to dictate exactly what they do inside the cage."

Our relative freedom of choice matters a great deal to Fowles because choosing between good and evil is the only way to stay human. He keeps looking for new terms to describe and extend this crucial relativism. The metaphor of the chess game in *The Magus* supplements that of the zoo, or menagerie, as a benchmark of free choice. Freedom must be used wisely. When bolstered by the cunning and foresight of the master chessplayer, it enlarges the realm of choice. Urfe says of Maurice Conchis, the first time the two men meet, "His eyes were those of a chessplayer who has made a good move," and later he calls Conchis "a chess master caught between two moves." The "obscure psychological chess" Conchis plays with him gains in intangibles what it forfeits in verifiable rewards. The game expands the players' skill and judgment. What happens on the board—the patterns of attack and defense, the feints and dodges of the pieces—counts more than any final result. Chess combines order and formality within the fluidity created by the many ways the chessmen can move. The game becomes its own object. The players obey both the rules and the physical limitations set by the board—the perimeter and the squares. These restrictions, though real, do not deny choice and enactment. The situation of the game allows plenty of scope for caution, boldness, and innovation.

The false sacrifice—losing a piece in order to take a more important piece from your opponent—runs through Fowles. Like prudence in Fielding's *Tom Jones,* this shrewdness is an acquired virtue that tempers the instinct. It is a virtue worth acquiring. Just as the chessplayer must plan several moves ahead, so are human goals best reached indirectly. The shortest distance between two points in the human sphere is not a straight line. Alternate options must be devised and kept alive, freeing us to devote more attention to details. Process supersedes product, and we become means oriented. The final outcome of life lies beyond our control. But if the whole adds to ten, we do have some say as to how we reach it. The whole is uncaring. It makes no difference if the parts comprising it are five and five or three and seven. So long as the sum is fixed at ten, the parts may change freely. Chaos only describes life to a point; physical law, causality, and free will also shape it. The "hazard within bounds" that gauges our movements keeps shifting.

This modified freedom is the best situation for mankind. At times, our lives cry out for order and ballast; at other time, the shell of routine gets too tight and we need to break out. Whichever way the Pirandellian balance swings, we must focus on nearest things. Since any moment can shift the overall balance, no detail can be scamped. Each act, like each move in a chess game, becomes supreme. *The Aristos* says a great deal about learning to appreciate details. Here is an instance:

> There are means-oriented societies, for whom the game is the game; and ends-oriented societies, for whom the game is winning . . . . The whole tendency of evolution and history suggests that man must become means-oriented if he is to survive.

Means-oriented behavior blocks all searches for absolute truth and ultimate reality. The following quotation from the German scientist and philosopher Ernst Mach (1836-1916) appears in both the revised and the original texts of *The Aristos:* "A piece of knowledge is never false or true—but only more or less biologically and evolutionally useful." Nothing has universal validity, even as a means. There is no single best method. Each situation creates its own problems and requires its own solution. Even the Aristos, the zenith of Fowles's creative evolutionism, cannot escape situational relativism. The term *Aristos* is adjectival rather than attributive or essential: "It is singular and means roughly 'the best for a given situation.'" The force of the Aristos does not go beyond the moment or the occasion. A solution to a special finite problem, the Aristos will give way to more evolved forms as the whole struggles to know and serve itself.

II

Nothing is intrinsically good or bad for Fowles. Fate and

free will, envy and happiness, even pleasure and pain, acquire value from their interplay and their context. Each is a process whose survival depends on the reality of its opposite. The pull of opposites is the mainspring of all creativeness, making for a singing, rippling tension rather than a stasis. This tension, in turn, instead of neutralizing conflict, turns conflict, Hegel-like, to higher ends and purposes.

This ontology is intrinsic, not imposed. The tug of counterforces defines reality. Reality is tensional in nature. Law, the organizing principle, and chaos, the disintegrating one, battle constantly, along with clash and resolution and also form and breakdown: "Anything that exists or can be imagined to exist is a pole. All feelings, ideas, thoughts are poles; and each pole has a counterpole." The definition even includes nonexistence, which counterweights and gives meaning to whatever exists.

Fowles's science of opposites resembles Hegel's, both in its scope and dualistic character. The inclusiveness of the two systems makes everything necessary and purposive. But, scything away the absolute, Fowles gains an open-endedness and flexibility that allow more play to human freedom. Although the universe may ignore human needs, man is best and happiest in a tensional situation. Opposition is beneficial. It must never be confused with the wish to destroy. What frustrates some can make others happy. Truth exists potentially in many places and comes from many combinations, convergences, and clashes. Though communism may want to annihilate its sworn enemy, capitalism, the two systems need each other for countersupport. Even happiness takes meaning from unhappiness: "We need insecurity, ugliness, evil, and pain" (*The Aristos*). These harsh realities drive us to their counterpoles—security, beauty, and pleasure. They give them their value and make them worth striving for. For this reason, man should not get everything he wants. If all wishes were fulfilled, most pleasures would be destroyed. Unfulfilled desire breeds dissatisfaction and thus aids progress by goading us to reason, imagine and compare. (The realm of "what might be" or "what might have happened" interests Fowles greatly.) Without the prod of frustration, stagnation and then boredom set in. Adam and Eve had all they wanted in the Garden of Eden, a perfect Paradise. What happened there proves God's wisdom in leaving some wishes unfulfilled. Had Paradise made Adam and Eve happy, they would not have gone out and found something to want: "The higher the standard of living, the greater the need for variety. The greater the leisure, the greater the lack of tension" (*The Aristos*). Not only progress, but life itself dries up without the tension of counterforces. Human survival depends on biological polarity. The sexual drive conditions man to think polarly, and the constant reminders of physical decay and death in man's midst tighten his grip on life.

Moments when life flares out in the proximity of death come often in Fowles. Miranda Grey strengthens both her moral and intellectual fiber while dying slowly in Clegg's cellar in *The Collector*. Surrounded by rotting flesh, Maurice Conchis, in *The Magus,* finds "the word 'being' no longer passive and descriptive, but active . . . almost imperative." Conchis himself drips death. His "leathery old skin" clings to his skull like a death mask, and he heightens his deathly look by wearing a water-polo cap. He also has heart trouble and, having been thrice buried, is believed dead by his townsfolk. The mortality swathing him affirms his centricity in the Godgame he holds every year to help others live fuller lives. In *The French Lieutenant's Woman,* natural landscape enters the tensional field. Flowers in the Undercliff, a wooded preserve near Lyme Regis, where most of the action takes place, bloom earlier than anywhere else in the area, and the flora grows to tropical density. This luxuriance comes from the erosion of the bedrock, which tips the land toward the sun.

Even the prosaic routine of daily living is tensional. The individual is a pole afloat in a sea of counterpoles. These he jostles without trying to change or destroy. Being, once again, has meaning in its own right; "to be" suffices for Fowles. Unlike Sartre, he is not threatened by *l'être pour-soi* (the being for self). That which exists outside the self is not gluey, nauseating, or hostile. Nor is it merely to be endured. It is necessary; it comforts, refreshes, and strengthens rather than tyrannizing or hedging in. The rhythmic interaction of the whole staves off the dead hand of stasis. To resonate in tune with the humming tension of counterpoles is to generate force. At a climactic moment in *The French Lieutenant's Woman,* Charles Smithson, the book's main character, rejoices to find himself on a level with ordinary experience and then rejoices again to find that experience both a miracle and an ecstasy:

> Charles's was the very opposite of the Sartrean experience. The simple furniture around him, the warm light from the next room, the humble shadows . . . were not encroaching and hostile objects, but constituting and friendly ones.

This refusal to see the world as flat and stale charges life with wonder; the most routine acts become exciting. Nicholas Urfe's happiest times in *The Magus* come during "moments when the most ordinary things seemed beautiful and lovable." The inexhaustibility of nature, far from nauseating us, humbles us. A reverence for natural process replaces the itch to tame or analyze nature. In a 1969 interview for *Life* magazine, Fowles said, "More and more I have been influenced by Zen Buddhist attitudes. What matters is the thing in itself." An article published in *Sports Illustrated* the following year extends the argument. Again he yokes passivity to a conceptless, priorityless view of nature: "As soon as we have a thing named, says Zen, we start forgetting about its real nature." He then attacks "the general human fault" of "naming things and then forgetting them": "The individual increasingly lets society and its label-words usurp his own role and responsibility." Fowles seeks no mystical union; nor does he addresses the inner planes of our minds. What he does do is to bestow equality on all living things and then revel in the equality. "Seeing and enjoying nature is infinitely more important than knowing how to name and analyze it,"[9] the essay continues. Fowles feels alive relaxing and enjoying his immediate surroundings. He is content that nature is available to be experienced and enjoyed.

The quiet civilized pleasure of enjoying appearances rests on faith and good will. To appreciate nature one cannot treat it as an object. The supreme lesson becomes to resist thinking beyond the moment. This lesson carries into Fowles's view of personal relationships. By looking to maximize the utility or profit-potential of whatever we confront, be it a tract of land or a personal relationship, people today make pleasure a duty. A subchapter of *The Aristos* called "The Monetization of Pleasure" discusses our inability "to conceive of pleasure except as being in some way connected with getting and spending." When having, and not being, dictates man's choices, he tries to extend his range of control to people. He turns all experiences and relationships into objects. Frederick Clegg, Fowles's collector, typifies this feature of capitalist society. But instead of accumulating property or cash, he collects girls. At the end of the book, he is looking over another girl to replace the one who died in his cellar. Girls have become interchangeable for him, like parts in a machine. His commodity fetish degrades and distorts sexual love. It is no wonder that he is sexless. When treated like a thing, sex becomes something to use and then throw away. The inner commitment that gives sex its meaning disappears. Maurice Conchis tells Urfe in *The Magus* that the abundance and

availability of sex today has robbed sex of much of its
romantic impact and beauty:

> You young people can lend your bodies now, play with them,
> give them as we [who grew up before World War I] could not. But
> remember that you have paid a price: that of a world rich in
> mystery and delicate emotion.

It takes Urfe more than four hundred pages to catch Conchis's
drift. What he learns is that the search for demonstrable
proofs defeats the moment and substitutes quantity for
quality. Like Clegg with his prisons, Urfe's sexual partners
had become interchangeable, and love was a lost gift. Looking
ahead to *The French Lieutenant's Woman,* Fowles describes
Urfe's new-found knowledge by comparing our era to the
Victorian:

> A young Victorian of my age would have thought nothing of
> waiting fifty months, let alone fifty days, for his beloved; and of
> never permitting a single unchaste thought to sully his mind.

The contrast between sexual attitudes today and in
Queen Victoria's time recurs more pointedly in *The French
Lieutenant's Woman.* As so often happens in the novel, the
contrast does not flatter us. The constant references to sex by
the advertising and entertainment media have blunted sex's
power to enchant:

> We are not so frustrated as the Victorians? Perhaps. But if you
> can only enjoy one apple a day, there's a great deal to be said
> against living in an orchard of the wretched things; you might
> even find apples sweeter if you were only allowed one a week.

Fowles's sexual dynamic owes much to Lawrence, especially
Lawrence's insistence that sexual love must respect both the

privacy and the "otherness" of the other person. Love is democratic, transcending any clutching for objective facts or tangible evidence. Gainsaying ownership, it works best when it leaves great tracts of the unexplored and unknown in both parties. Urfe's relationship with Alison Kelly validates Conchis's belief, "Love is the mystery between two people, not the identity." It thrives on mystery. Alison's uniqueness defies classification, her indwelling resistance to categories and label-terms making her exciting. By saying of her, "She was bizarre, a kind of human oxymoron," Urfe confers life upon her. He refers to her half-Australian and half-British speech and calls her "innocent-corrupt, coarse-fine, an expert novice." Even her looks bypass ordinary standards: "She would be ugly one moment, and then some movement, look, angle of her face, made ugliness impossible." Sarah Woodruff in *The French Lieutenant's Woman* also comes alive because of the stir her unclassifiability rouses in Charles Smithson. Again, being operates inversely with knowing and naming. She is "luring-receding, subtle-simple, proud-begging, defending-accusing." Rejoicing in her gossamer uniqueness, Charles tells her, "You are both so close and yet a stranger." That she is, is everything to him.

The life-giving power of mystery floods all of reality. Mystery squares well with Fowles's definition of man as a seeker, or "everlack"; by discouraging the search for final explanations, it promotes means-oriented thinking. Again, the idea rings of D.H. Lawrence, and, again, its best spokesman in Fowles is Maurice Conchis. "Mystery has energy," says Conchis. "It pour energy into whoever seeks the answer to it. If you disclose the solution to the mystery, you are simply depriving the other seekers . . . of an important source of energy." The existence of mysteries is more important than their solution because solutions block thought.

To keep ourselves alert and nimble-witted we need all the mystery we can get. "Mirage," a 1960 poem by Fowles based on Chekhov's *The Three Sisters,* contrasts the glamor of the faraway with the drabness of the readily available. What is known stales; that which the mind cannot compass, on the other hand, gleams and beckons. The "desert-making heresy / That happiness is having what one lacks" stems from "our hated and familiar nows."[10] The three Prozorov sisters in Chekhov's play view Moscow as an earthly paradise. Moscow outshines everything else. Even though it can be as crass as the most provincial backwater, it stands as the sum of the sisters' hopes. These hopes, it needs reminding, do not sour because the sisters never go to Moscow. That Moscow never sinks to the drab prose of material fact brightens, rather than dims, its luster.

If mystery is synonymous with ignorance, it shares little with helplessness or frustration. The absence of certainty refocuses our efforts. Man stops fighting the truth that reality is fundamentally mysterious and starts to work with, rather than against, nature. Learning to cope does not overlook life's variety, freshness, and surprise. Mystery accepts chance, or hazard, as a key principle of life. To survive, man needs a plan, and whatever plan it be must center on chance. Life is a network of chance. Free will, physical law, and evolution are all governed by chance. Chance, or hazard, though, works indifferently, dispersing itself among humanity at random. It does not always bring misfortune, as in Fowles's hero, Thomas Hardy. Sometimes it helps. Either way, though, it exerts great force. Maurice Conchis says, "Hazard makes you elect; you cannot elect yourself." The universal parity of existence holds no special brief for man; the whole has no favorites. Hazard demands that options be kept open. By recognizing this, we can limit hazard's dangers and make the most of its benefits. We learn to shake off trouble and to use our good luck before it sours or goes away. The hazard-free situation Clegg works toward during Miranda's captivity denies reality, bringing about her *physical* and his *moral* death. Conchis tells how hazard led him to the acreage he has occupied and carved a life from for the past twenty-four years:

> I came to Phraxos looking for a house to rent . . . . On my last day I had a boatsman take me around the island. For pleasure. By chance he landed me for a swim at Moutsa down there. By chance he said there was an old cottage up here. By chance I came up.

Chance also rules in *The French Lieutenant's Woman.* Charles Smithson tells Sarah Woodruff, "I am rich by chance, you are poor by chance." He speaks more wisely than he knows. He and Sarah serve evolution for the same reason that Conchis directs the Godgame energizing *The Magus:* all three characters cooperate with hazard. Adaption aids survival and evolution. To emphasize the point, the last chapter of *The French Lieutenant's Woman* takes as its epigraph the following excerpt from Martin Gardner's *The Ambidextrous Universe* (1967): "Evolution is simply the process by which chance . . . cooperates with natural law to create living forms better and better adapted to survive." Hazard counterweights the planned, the known, and the formalized. This potency makes it our most important tool for experiment and improvisation. We must welcome it in order to expand to full growth.

III

A minor character in *The French Lieutenant's Woman* says offhandedly, "Now that's what a woman does. Makes you see what's in front of your nose." The throwaway remark says a good deal about Fowles. In a 1970 review of Angus Wilson's *The World of Charles Dickens,* he chided Dickens for "an almost complete inability to invent intelligent, independent women." [11] One reason for his admiration of his fellow Dorsetman, Thomas Hardy, is Hardy's feminism. Hardy and Meredith are probably the only Victorian novelists whose female characters have healthier instincts than their male counterparts. Fowles's belief in woman's clarity and creativity matches that of Meredith and Hardy. Women in Fowles not only make men see what is under their noses; they also see deeper purposes and more loving uses for the prerogatives men almost always usurp:

> My female characters [Fowles said in 1968] tend to dominate the male. I see man as a kind of artifice, and woman as a kind of reality. The one is cold idea, the other is warm fact . . . . If the technical problems hadn't been so great, I should have liked to make Conchis in **The Magus** a woman. [12]

This tribute to Conchis makes it fitting that the key statement on Fowles's feminism come from Conchis:

> Men love war . . . . In it they can reduce women to the status of objects. That is the great distinction between the sexes. Men see objects, women see the relationship between objects.

Conchis excepted, none of Fowles's male characters knows how to conduct a warm human relationship. None wants to share or commit himself. None can separate love from social prejudice. Clegg has no moral or sexual passion, only a social inferiority complex. Urfe, accustomed to gorging himself sexually, clears out of any sexual relationship as soon as it threatens his freedom. Charles Smithson, though just as frightened as Urfe of a close tie with a woman, does not indulge himself sexually. He is too timid and bystanderish. Living in an age evasive of sex, he subordinates erotic love to sentimental notions about duty. It is apt that the sexual disorientation of Clegg, Urfe, and Smithson should show so vividly in their sexual performances. Clegg cannot have sex with a women; Urfe is told by Alison Kelly that he is not the best lover she has known; Smithson wears a shirt during sex and usually goes to church afterwards to repent.

The psychological difference between men and women is stated in *The Aristos:* "Women know more about human nature, more about mystery, and more about keeping passion alive." As Conchis said, they are better at relationships than men. Any close human tie needs sexual and psychological separation at times for the sake of relief. Women's ability to assess a relationship empowers them to foresee which risks it can afford, when to take the risks, and how to use the risks to strengthen the relationship. Women know the romantic value of separation better than men because of menstruation, which renews married sex with added force on account of the break in sexual routine it imposes. And since women menstruate and not men, the wife can interpret her peiod in line with the psychosexual needs of the marriage at any time.

Also explainable biologically is woman's greater capacity for faith and imagination. This capacity includes religious piety, self-confidence, and the good-natured belief that relationships bring more joy than sorrow. Instead of intellectualizing love or fleeing it, women accept it as something to be enjoyed. Sexual realists as well as optimists, they let love grow in its own way, and they welcome love's renewals rather than bemoaning its limits. Their intuitive knowledge that love is a giving without return teaches them not to ask too much of love. Charles Smithson startles to hear his fiancee say, in the scene where he breaks their engagement, that her love for him overrides his weak character. Smithson is unequipped—perhaps biologically—to understand such generosity. And with good reason: the commitment to unrevealed life characterizing the maternal instinct and woman's higher threshold of pain signal a maturity and unselfishness few men can match. These gifts express themselves intuitively in women, forming a large part of women's gift to humanity. Women respect life as a fluid process. They are more innovative and imaginative than men because their intuitive grasp of process outweighs the need for proofs. A character in *The Magus* predicts, "One day all our great practicing . . . psychiatrists will be of the sex of Eve." Fowles does not test the prediction. His female characters do show, though, that the masculine ethic of capitalism that rules the present age needs an infusion of the feminine virtues of intuition, subtlety, and experiment. Unless a society learns to balance male and female principles, it cannot grow into a civilization. England's collapse from empire to commonwealth and the emergence of fascism, imperialism's child, in this age both go back to the iron, man-centered ethos of nineteenth-century industrialism.

Statecraft today has little patience with the female spirit. The two chief duties of government in our time, as Fowles sees them, are to educate and depopulate. The introduction of women into key governmental roles might help expedite these tasks. The tasks, it hardly needs saying, cry out for immediate attention: "Overpopulation breeds famine, war, disease, misery, frustration; and it breeds . . . ignorance," Fowles says in *The Aristos*. Ignorance, in turn, causes inequality of wealth and also of the means by which wealth is obtained—educational opportunity. The poor cannot lawfully better themselves. "One cause of all crime is maleducation," he continues. A better education would have removed Clegg's need to kidnap Miranda Grey. Kidnapping is the only outlet the state has left him for exercising political choice. But if Clegg's freedom of speech has shrunk to a matter of kidnapping, then the state wants help. Clegg does not need power over another person. What he does need is schooling. He must learn to govern himself—to work out his freedom in the light of other freedoms. But overpopulation has herded him into a slum, taught him no craft, and denied him the self-respect that goes with learning a skill. Education is a tool, a resource, and a social activity. It must be loose limbed enough to meet many needs. Ultimately, it readies man for his evolutionary task; it cannot afford to teach subjects because they are theoretically attractive or politically popular. Too much is at stake. In order to serve the needs of freedom, justice, and mind, education to respect the individual. But attention to individuals is precisely where education scores lowest. Education is controlled by the state, and the state, like all organizations, seeks above all to keep itself alive. It frowns on education because true education— the twin discoveries of self and state—opposes the status quo. The state rewards the conformist more than the innovator. The most successful, well-adjusted citizens in the West today want to prolong the state as it is.

Fowles's views on education and politics, while biting and colorful, have a shaky underpinning. Because of the uneven way he states them, they are opinions but not a program. He wants to reform education and he explains why educational reform is needed. He opts for a supple, revisionist politics that both respects hazard and gives women a creative role. Though not pretending that everybody is born equal, he wants everybody to have equal rights and opportunities, especially in the area of education. How, though, are these reforms to be implemented? Who will carry them out? The nearest he comes to an answer is to recommend democratic socialism in *The Aristos* as "the only rational political doctrine." Yet he quickly takes back his recommendation. Though "total inequality of wealth, our present condition, is unsatisfactory . . . comparative equality of wealth . . . is full of danger." Initiative and incentive suffer, and a facile egalitarianism governs political choice. People have no room in which to grow. The Aristos starves for want of a cause. But even *he* is too sketchy to be taken seriously. A radical individualist, he may be worth 10,000 others. But how did he attain this stature? How does his merit help others? In which situations is he most effective? *The Aristos* leaves an embarrassing gap between its eponym's self-development and public utility. Nor does an Aristos turn up in the novels. Until he makes himself known, his strength and worth cannot be judged.

IV

Though roughly formulated, Fowles's politics never stiffen to romantic posturing. Born in 1926, John Fowles is still in his early maturity, and whatever insights the years bring need not concern us here. He is a literary artist and must be judged, finally, on aesthetic grounds. He published his first book, *The Collector,* at age thirty-seven after abandoning several others in varying degrees of completion. His aesthetic preachments make clear his hesitancy to rush into print. Art must prepare man for his evolutionary responsibility, and any work in progress that falls below this requirement must be scrapped.

The artist's role springs from the tension generated between art and its counterpole, science. Fowles's existential-ism, like most other kinds, inheres in choice—the ability to make unscientific judgments and to know right from wrong. Science, for all its measuring tools, cannot help here. In decision-making, help comes only from philosophy and the arts. Nowadays in particular, science has grown so complex that it requires intense specialization. This specialization, though necessary, turns the scientist into an applied techni-cian, clouding his view of the human context that gives his work its meaning. If science disembodies, says Fowles in *The*

Aristos, then art must embody and make whole:

> The scientist atomizes, someone must synthesize; the scientist
> withdraws, someone must draw together. The scientist particu-
> larizes, someone must universalize.

Art condenses, whereas science merely abstracts, because of
art's broader, more humane scope. Hazard and the feminine
virtues of intuition and compassion have little place in science.
In fact, they blur the objectivity science needs to do its
analytical work. Art, on the other hand, probes that layer of
life that defies calculation:

> Art, even the simplest, is the expression of truths too complex for
> science to express, or to conveniently express. This is not to say
> that science is in some way inferior to art, but that they have
> different purposes and different uses.

Art's eagerness to face mystery and hazard, which cramp
science, gives art a topicality and universality science cannot
match. Whereas a scientific discovery of a century ago has
chiefly antiquarian interest today, a novel or play written then
can still refresh and strengthen. The artist can rise above the
moment because he is a person speaking to other people
rather than to a specialist. He is one of ours, differing from
us only in the extent of his sensitivity. In *The Magus,* Fowles
uses Parnassus, the shrine of Apollo and the Muses, to
symbolize a height that, while awesome, can be scaled step by
human step. The symbolic lesson of Parnassus is warmly
human: if we cannot produce great art, we can still appreciate
it. *The Aristos* joins the artist to the human community at
large by citing the gregariousness and inclusiveness of art:

> To be an artist is not to be a member of a secret society; it is not an
> activity forbidden to the majority of mankind . . . . We are not all
> to be Leonardos; but of the same kind as Leonardo, for genius is
> only one end of the scale.

The artist reaches outward and probes inward at the same time, carefully maintaining a balance between the demands of psychic and material reality:

> His [the artist's] simplest purpose is to describe the outer world; his next is to express his feelings about that outer world, and his last is to express his feelings about himself.

Representational art has lost ground in our century to the romantic cult of feeling. Fowles tries to redress this shift in emphasis by couching *The French Lieutenant's Woman* in a Victorian idiom; better to go too far in the direction of naturalism than in that of psychological analysis. The cult of personal uniqueness either neglects its audiences or adopts the elitist attitude that its audience needs to be taught, not entertained. It has also ushered in a glorification of style for its own sake. To certify their uniqueness, artists everywhere today seek the distinguishing style and stance. Their excessive preoccupation with manner devalues thought. Expression dominates what is expressed, and the deathly offspring of stylistic extravagance—decadence—rules the field. *Polystylism,* on the other hand, denotes real artistry, celebrating the refusal of genius to stay locked within a single idiom. A real master asserts both his freedom and technical control by breaking out of the false security of a manner. Thus Fowles, by writing *The Collector* in antiphonal voices, gains access to the psyches, private histories, and value systems of two sharply different characters. That each character also differs sharply from Fowles himself betokens compassion and self-detachment as well as a stylistic triumph. The idea that freedom must enact itself in a sea of counterpointing freedoms applies rigorously to art. The best art exults in differing life styles and modes of being. Rather than cutting Miranda and Clegg to a thesis, Fowles gives them the freedom of their own perceptions, vocabulary, and syntax. Freeing character from the control of plot makes the novelist's job harder, but it creates a richer, more exciting picture. This freedom cannot happen in a vacuum. As Fowles's definition of the artist's purpose says, it must account for external reality. Fowles heightens character by projecting it against a living background. The background is ultimately English. Miranda says in her diary in *The Collector* that art reflects a tradition of national culture: "You accept that you are English. you don't pretend that you'd rather be French or Italian or something else." Fowles repeated the same argument to Roy Newquist, stressing the practice of novel-writing: "We need a return to the great tradition of the English novel—realism. English is a naturally empirical language; I suppose that's why realism haunts all our arts." Although Fowles's ideas and settings shatter national borders, his main characters are always English. The hugely theatrical Godgame that touches scores of lives in *The Magus* ends prosaically in a London park. Fowles does not overreach himself. Though he has lived in France and Greece, his books always express English life. English life is shaped to his hand. He knows England, not as a mental datum, but as lived-with fact. He responds to it instinctively as well as intellectually. No sentimentality or quaintness mars his view of the English. His organic response to his countrymen gives his most abstruse remarks about England immediacy and drive. Bypassing cleverness, it also has the powerful unifying effect of fusing literary and social tradition.

Fowles's passion for occupying center stage in his books has already been noted.[13] His literary opinions support the claim that he puts a lot of himself into his fiction. The critic has to reveal the person behind the writer to comprehend the works. J. Hillis Miller's *Thomas Hardy: Distance and Desire* (1970) neglects Hardy's personal life and thus gives an incomplete picture of its subject; "*Why* was Hardy like this?"

Fowles asks. "What *did* happen in his real life . . .? Why did his first marriage sour so disastrously fast? What real-life factors structured his literary pessimism?"[14] The following digression from *The French Lieutenant's Woman* again claims that for Fowles the biographical reading of literature tells most about the composition and formation of an author's mind:

> If we want to know the real Mill or the real Hardy, we can learn more from the deletions and alterations of their biographies than from the published versions . . . more from correspondence that somehow escaped burning, from private diaries, from the petty detritus of the concealment operation.

The concealment operation does not play a big part in Fowles. He does not cover his tracks or lay false trails; his putting himself at the heart of his novels removes the need for literary detection. He admits that Charles Smithson, the main character of *The French Lieutenant's Woman,* might be himself disguised; like Nicholas Urfe of *The Magus,* he taught English unconscientiously in Greece; personal interviews in both *Life* and the *New York Times Book Review* reveal that he once shared Frederick Clegg's passion for collecting butterflies.[15] This tie between Fowles and his nastiest character makes good the point that Fowles writes from his own experience. The obsession with collecting stabs out of all his books. Had he not shared the obsession, he could not have portrayed his collector so chillingly. Had he not loathed the collector in himself, he would not keep returning to the obsession in the hope of exorcising it. A need to confess and purge guilt explains much of *The Collector's* jolt. Ritual runs high in autobiographical novelists. When they can use it to ease the hurt of voicing painful self-truths, they seize the chance. It gives them the objectivity and form necessary for artistic distancing. In so doing, it creates an opportunity to approach, convey, and symbolize a reality too painful to cope with otherwise.

But why should Fowles use prose narrative as his means of self-expression? Formal ritual has just as much reality in poetry, music, or sculpture as in fiction. What gives fiction its advantage over its sister arts? These questions are nearly unanswerable. Since artists are seized by their media, any answer may tell more about the creator than about his creations, more about Fowles himself than about his fiction. The teacher in Fowles, though, needs words to point morals, to persuade, and to develop ties between ideas. "The word is man's most precise and inclusive tool," he says in *The Aristos.* Because literature uses words, it is the queen of the arts. The visual arts describe appearances more vividly, and music expresses emotion better than words. These arts also communicate with a speed and convenience beyond the powers of literature. But they fail to reveal what underlies appearance. Lacking the bite and subtlety of words, they cannot deliver the same accuracy and quantity of information as literature. Literature's domain is experience that cannot be summarized and defined; literature reveals depths and shadings not found in the other arts. A Mozart sonata may describe Mozart's sadness with stark immediacy. But only words can knife to the cause and meaning of the sadness. A biography—because it is made up of words—will tell more about Mozart than any number of sonatas.

Fowles's awareness of the uses of language floods his books. Rhetorically, he is a classicist, dealing with ideas formally and peppering his work with learned allusions from all fields. He gains his effects through conscious execution. Bypassing devices like incoherence and redundancy, he makes his points with apt, economical dialogue, rhythmically expanding symbols, and shapely narrative structure. This classicism puts him in a modern as opposed to a contemporary tradition. Whereas the subcellar people of Sartre, Beckett, and Pinter find reality sticky and sluggish, Fowles's characters try to make sense of it. The modern scorns both antirationalism and submissiveness. He is intellectual, formal, and corrective. He laces his didacticism with enormous erudition: the syncretism of Yeats, the interlingual puns and homophones of Joyce's cosmic comedy, the cultural dovetailings of *The Waste Land*. Fowles's commitment to reason, coherence, and social reform through education puts him in this tradition; *The French Lieutenant's Woman* contains the suggestion that its author is "trying to pass off a concealed book of essays" in the garb of fiction. Yet this and his other novels sell well and make successful movies. His popularity proves that he is neither speaking to an elite nor using fiction simply to preach moral instruction. He is a wonderful entertainer whose joy in living allows him to delight and instruct simultaneously. His routine descriptions throb with poetic intensity, and his characters' most random encounters spur thought. These moments—grounded in a belief in the supremacy of individual freedom—command the public's attention. Fowles rings many exciting changes on his commitment; all of them have the jolt, heft, and resonance of major fiction.

NOTES TO CHAPTER 1

1. John Fowles, "Notes on an Unfinished Novel," in *Afterwords: Novelists on Their Novels*, ed. Thomas McCormack (New York and Evanston, Ill.: Harper & Row, 1969), p. 169.
2. Roy Newquist, ed., "John Fowles," *Counterpoint* (New York: Simon and Schuster, 1964), p. 220.
3. Ibid., pp. 222, 224.
4. Joyce Carol Oates, "A Novelist's World: Ceremonial, Absurd, and Real," *Book World*, 2 November 1969, 3.
5. Richard Boston, "John Fowles, Alone But Not Lonely," New York

Times Book Review, 9 November 1969, p. 2.

6. Robert Scholes, "The Orgiastic Fiction of John Fowles," *The Hollins Critic* 6(December 1969): 3; Marvin Mudrick, "Evelyn, Get the Horseradish," *Hudson review* 19 (Summer 1966): 305.

7. John Fowles, "Thomas Hardy: Distance and Desire," *New York Times Book Review,* 21 June 1970, p. 4.

8. Newquist, p. 225

9. Richard B. Stolley, "The French Lieutenant's Woman's Man: Novelist John Fowles," *Life,* 29 May 1970, p. 60; John Fowles, "Weeds, Bugs, Americans," *Sports Illustrated,* 21 December 1970, pp. 86, 99, 102, 99.

10. John Fowles, "Mirage," *Antaeus* 1 (Summer 1970): 22.

11. John Fowles, "Guide to a Man-Made Planet," *Life,* 4 September 1970, p. 8.

12. Fowles, "Notes . . . ," p. 172.

13. *See* note 1, above.

14. Fowles, "Thomas Hardy. . . . ," p. 4.

15. Boston, p. 52; Stolley, p. 60.

2
Revolt from the Gutter

The Collector (1963) tells the story of a clerk who wins £ 73,000 in a football pool and then kidnaps a young art student, whom he holds prisoner in his cellar till her death. The clerk has no friends, feels strongly about nothing, lacks a sense of humor, and displays no sexual force. His language is stiff and stale; badly educated and void of ideas, he cannot conceive of anything existing beyond his whims. He has never voted, had sex, nor lived away from home except for his military service. He holds too low an opinion of himself to attempt growth—moral, intellectual, or spiritual. In the words of his prisoner, Miranda Grey, he is "an empty space disguised as a human" and "a sea of cotton wool."

Out of this shriveled subject matter, Fowles paints one of modern literature's best portraits of a weak man. He describes Frederick Clegg's weakness, shows it effects on others, and explores both the psychological and historical realities that brought it about. Clegg's memoir gives Clegg pure and unadorned; he has nothing to give and he learns nothing. Fowles's feat of making him both predictable and chilling gains force from the novel's continuity. As soon as Miranda is captured, the reader fears for her, and his worst fears are realized. On the second day of her imprisonment, she tells Clegg, "You see I'm miserable. The air, I can't breathe at nights, I've woken up with a headache. I should die if you kept me here long." What she predicts, happens: Clegg holds her in the cellar, and, denied fresh air and sunshine, she dies within two months. Thus Fowles gets his main ideas and dramatic tensions out early and sees them through rigorously. But in the process he destroys plot, story, and suspense. In their place he poses the questions of how and when Miranda will discover what is happening. The challenge he gives himself in *The Collector* is enormous. So long as Miranda remains a captive, her life brings no change or hope. No action depends on an earlier action. The book goes nowhere. It is contained, actionless, and without motion. Because Clegg has blocked sequence, each event exists for itself. He has no plan. He keeps Miranda prisoner in order to keep her prisoner. He backs the status quo; though she gives him nothing, he wants to prolong her imprisonment as long as he can. No issue builds between them. The only action he takes—besides restraining her—is to disavow action.

How, then, does Fowles hold our attention? How can he bypass so many of the resources of prose narrative and still keep us turning pages? Even though he handicaps himself, he has no symptoms of artistic cramp. He does not grope, cheat, or force conclusions. Incidents convey meaning, and these he develops with power and craft. Miranda says at one point, "This isn't just a fantastic situation; it's a fantastic variation of a fantastic situation." Fowles's inventiveness thrums so sharply—even in a first novel—that only composite terms like realist-fantasist or empiricist-illusionist can compass it. *The Collector* is a fantasy told in precise, realistic details. "Believability must dominate even the most outlandish situation," Fowles said in 1964: "For me the obligation is to present my characters realistically. They must be credible human beings even if the circumstances they are in are 'incredible.'" Defoe merits praise because of his ability to ground a fantastic situation in plausibility:

I must write in terms of strict realism. I'm a great admirer of Daniel Defoe—what I admire most is his creation of the extremely unusual situation, such as we find in **Robinson Crusoe,** treated scrupulously in terms of his talent and honestly in terms of life. [1]

Wildly original novels like *Robinson Crusoe* (which is mentioned in *The Magus*) and Golding's *Lord of the Flies* do not break loose from realism. Like them, *The Collector* succeeds because of its vision, its truth to human motives, and its workmanly narrative technique.

The Collector explores human possibilities. To grant it plausibility is to raise questions that probe a universal level of consequence. Does Clegg's willingness to give Miranda anything but freedom bring her situation close to ours? And while Clegg shows that lethal people exist *around* us, does he not also touch something lethal *within* us? Though his need for security through love takes demented forms, the need is universal, and all of us have been driven to unreason by it. The plausibility of *The Collector* goes beyond technique. It gives a long, many-sided look at human reality.

I

Though Frederick Clegg likes being called Ferdinand, he does not live up to the princely virtues (from *The Tempest*) connected with his chosen name. One must go to his last name to understand him. *Cleg* is a dialect word in England for a sluggish and vampirish horsefly. The dull, wooden name of Clegg also characterizes him in the larger context of Western tradition. The phonetic similarity between it and the modern French word for *key* (*clef*) describes him as Miranda's turnkey or jailer; a key is also a system for labeling or classifying biological relationships. Though entomology, Clegg's hobby, is an arm of biology, he has no relationships. The likeness between *clef* and Old English *clegg* (pronounced, *clay*) mirrors this incapacity. Miranda's bright beauty is mired in clay. The common clay that forms Fowles's collector represents a new limit for naturalism. As in the paintings of Ivan Albright, Joyce's *Ulysses*, and Hubert Selby's *Last Exit to Brooklyn*, he is so ordinary that he is extraordinary.

Fowles knows that if the commonplace can cause wonder, it can also unleash terror and shock. He says in *The Aristos*, "The ordinary man is the curse of civilization," and he told Roy Newquist, "I think the common man is the curse of civilization, not its crowning glory. And he needs education, not adulation. The boy in *The Collector* stands for the Many; the girl for the Few." [2] These terms need defining. The Newquist interview goes on to develop the idea, from Heraclitus, that mankind is split into two camps—the Few, a moral and intellectual elite, and the Many, or hoi polloi, the mindless, conforming majority. *The Collector* turns on the statistical and biological fact that independent, creative people have always been outnumbered by their apathetic counterparts. These, the Many, have distrusted and resented the Few because of their resistance to easy, prefabricated moralities. Unashamedly didactic, Fowles calls *The Collector* a parable whose point is that we must build a society where the Few can live freely and teach the Many. Clegg's capture of Miranda is an act of revenge, spurred by class difference. But Clegg does not need to play the avenger. Fowles dislikes the contemporary ideal of the inarticulate hero, based on Salinger's Holden Caulfield (*Catcher in the Rye*) and Sillitoe's Arthur Seaton (*Saturday Night and Sunday Morning*). Overgrown maladjusted adolescents like these need schooling, not power or vengeance. Fowles's remarks to Newquist show that he geared *The Collector* to the double requirements of topicality and timelessness: "What I tried to say in the book was this . . . In societies dominated by the Many, the Few are in grave danger of being suffocated. This is why the Many often seems like a terrible tyranny."[3]

Fowles's view of the "biologically irrefutable" split between Few and Many goes past Heraclitus. Forces like chance, heredity, and environment condition the split. Often, a person cannot choose to belong to the Few or the Many. Nor is the Few-Many division always clearly marked. Everybody has in him elements from both strains, even the Aristos, Fowles's most fully developed human. The 1970 edition of *The Aristos* presents the division as a spectrum rather than a split: "The gradations are infinite . . . *the dividing line between the Few and the Many must run through each individual, not between individuals.* In short none of us are wholly perfect; and none wholly imperfect." Fowles does not find these gradations upsetting; he delights in unpredictability and surprise. The playful reference to Dizzystone and Gladraeli in *The French Lieutenant's Woman,* while not new, describes tersely Victorian England's two great statesmen taking atypical stands. Clegg and Miranda, too, though they never switch roles, sometimes display traits more characteristic of their opposite than of themselves. The inconsistency is deliberate, for it both humanizes the clash between Clegg and Miranda and gives the action a realistic moral reference.

Before looking into moral complexities, though, we have to review Clegg's suitability as an archetype of the common man and also the particular threat posed by his commonness in our day. As seen in *Saturday Night and Sunday Morning,* blue-collar workers in England enjoyed more freedom in the 1950s than ever before. The New People, as Miranda calls them, often had television sets, motorcycles, and flashy wardrobes of teddy-boy clothes. Though Clegg is no factory hand, he does come from the working class and shares some of their faults. He resents people with more education or money

than he has, and he does not use his freedom well. Relieved of
the burden of supporting himself, he is independent but also
rudderless. *The Collector* tests a social nostrum from *The
Aristos,* that is, that "the twentieth century's happy man is the
man with money." Money and the responsibilities it brings
create challenges beyond Clegg's powers. Not only does his
luck deny the equation of wealth and happiness. Though it
frees him from a boring job, it brings out the worst traits in
him, as well as in his aunt, his cousin, the real-estate man who
sells him the house where he stows Miranda, and also in the
decorators and furnishers who get the house ready ("everyone
fleeced me"). His class consciousness spoils his outing to a
London restaurant, where he goes to celebrate his winnings.
To raise his spirits, he goes to a prostitute; but, unable to have
sex, he feels still more depressed and left out. The separating
and corrupting effects of money go through him as through
water. He leaves his job and gives up all his personal ties. He
collects his winnings and buys a camera, "the best, telephoto
lens," which he uses to take pornographic photos. He is
cruelly reminded of his social and sexual inadequacies. He
becomes a snob, saying of his aunt and cousin, with whom he
has lived since age two, "You could see what they were at
once, even more than me . . . small people who'd never left
home." Then he kidnaps Miranda.

None of these acts is free. What he wants keeps clashing
with what he does. He finds himself continually going against
his wishes, interests, and comforts, and he never understands
his conduct well enough to change it. He had wanted a new
house but buys an old one. He says of Miranda, "I would do
anything to know her, to please her, to be her friend." Yet
capturing her defeats these hopes. From the outset he is
trapped; whatever he does turns out wrong: "I was drawn
in . . . against my will almost"; "I didn't want to kill her, that
was the last thing I wanted." This failure shows clearly in his

first conversation with Miranda. "My mind was really quick that morning," he recalls. But he is easily ruffled and routed. On the next page he says, "I knew what I said was confused." That Miranda, recently chloroformed and kidnapped, is both sick and shocked degrades Clegg still more. He shrinks quickly. Like the self-division hinted at by his chosen name, Ferdinand Clegg, and the omission of quotation marks around his speeches in his memoir, Miranda's easy rout nearly whips him out of reality altogether.

Other people invigorate Miranda, but they inhibit him. He has been hemmed in so long that when a beautiful girl comes his way he gets confused and then kills her. He lacks the self-acceptance, intelligence, and information to have a human relationship. A product of capitalism, he shrills at Miranda, "Tell me what you want, I'll buy you anything." Money, his words imply, solves all problems. His money *has* created a perfect society; all his needs are filled and nobody else's opinion counts. But he and Miranda are bored stiff. Because it is unnatural, his society of one is doomed; hazard, mystery, and the responsibility of nourishing human ties must infuse all social arrangements. A 1963 poem by Fowles, "In Paradise," records the futility of blocking change. The poem, a chain of one-line remarks in dialogue, begins with, "So charming to meet you," and, "Heavenly evening," and ends with the word, "Goodbye," recited three times.[4] Though Clegg's facile identification of money, power, and happiness comes to grief, *The Collector* sustains no quarrel with capitalism. The variety and leisure that money brings are worthwhile. But they need to be shared, not hoarded.

Clegg's background proves him not fully accountable for his crimes. None of the forces that led him to kidnap Miranda has prepared him to deal with her. Many of them, in fact, were outside his control—his genes, his social class, his maleducation. Clegg suffers from what Fowles calls a *pawn complex.* He has no sense of importance; his *individuality* menaced. *The Aristos* calls this anxiety the *Nemo,* "The state of being nobody—'nobodiness.'" It comes from comparing oneself unfavorably to others. Though vexing, the practice is useful. It brings to mind the inequality of existence, and, along with its counterpole, the ego, aids independence of judgment and freedom of action. It helps evolution. Unfortunately, the threat of nonentity also disconcerts. Whereas we preen and prettify the ego, the Nemo brings panic. We are terrified by our ephemerality. We must cheat the Nemo.

This compulsion has had ruinous effects. The need for identity and security has exalted action; action is the best way to hold the Nemo at bay. Man substitutes action for security. Anybody threatened by ephemerality will prefer action over plain good conduct, because action attracts more notice. But the creed of action for action's sake blunts moral values and spurs a desperate search for uniqueness; adultery increases, possessions pile up, and the tempo of life quickens. Since the end of World War II, the Many have used the tape recorder and the camera to stave off the Nemo. In a society where ownership confers personal worth, reproducing an event on film or tape adds to a person's stature; it is as if the person has stopped time to own or multiply the event. But the prevalence of pseudoscientific devices like the camera and tape recorder has cheapened science. No enemy of science, Fowles calls scientific method "the linchpin, the axis of reason" (*The Aristos*), and he wants everybody to learn it. Today's consumer state, though, has turned the scientist into an applied technician. Instead of teaching scientific method, he is encouraged to train mechanics. The social pressures exerted by the Nemo have robbed him of his role as a discoverer or adventurer. Content or substance always takes precedence in Fowles over form. As soon as style, surface, and visual appeal encroach on content, mechanical values drive out organic ones. This trend has gained force since 1945, and Clegg is the product of it. His photography and butterfly collection negate mystery. They deny change and chance. They have made Clegg both a commodity-fetishist and, as Miranda says, a "visual." To delve beneath surfaces would be to go against the spirit of his society. A weak person, Clegg does not learn to cope with profundity or uniqueness. Nearly all his values are collective. His inarticulateness, rather than betokening a James Dean-like nobility, signals a dreary conformity and a failure in both imagination and depth. It also makes him very dull company.

One force that shriveled him was the home he grew up in. His father, a commercial traveler, died after a drunk-driving spree when Clegg was only two. Then his tippling mother left home with her lover, abandoning her son to his aunt and uncle. The uncle died during a fishing outing when Clegg was fifteen. The uncle's name, Dick, and his dying among fishing rods symbolize the end of Clegg's maleness. From this point, he grows up in a home without a man to emulate or identify with. Lacking this healthful influence, he becomes twisted, especially in his attitude toward women. His Aunt Annie and her invalid daughter Mabel he resents for their shabby-genteel narrowness, just as he resents his mother for her moral vagrancy. Privileged people he learns to resent because of his family's low-church ties. So after he sends his aunt and cousin to Australia, he is free to vent his social and sexual wrath on Miranda.

He tells Miranda that he was never punished as a schoolboy, and he usually wears a hangdog look the reverse of wrathful energy. Yet the only thing that kept him decent as a boy and young man was his obscurity. What he does after he becomes rich makes one ask whether more of his kind of madness would prevail if more people had the opportunity. Miranda is right to call him "a perfect example of petit-bourgeois squareness." Had he ever rebelled against family and church, he might not have killed Miranda. Her attempts to help him cannot lift him above his slum mentality. What he cannot solve or cope with is her individuality—as a person, a mind, and a channel of communication. Her beauty and surprise first confuse and then anger him. He only goes to touch her—except for restraining her—when she is either unconscious or dead. So beauty-starved and self-distrustful is he that he degrades all attempts at communication. He keeps crawling beneath her. Flattery will not lower his guard because he lacks both the imagination and self-respect to accept flattery. His low opinion of himself blocks interchange. Lacking humanity, he cannot perceive it in others; his habit is to degrade all motives. Perhaps his pathological fear of sex stems from sex's democratic nature. Miranda's sexual overture drives a wedge between them so great that it divides them completely. "We've been naked in front of each other," she tells him after their failed attempt at sex. "We can't be further apart." Their relationship tailspins quickly after this episode: motives clash more openly, hostility mounts, and she dies in less than a month.

The only way she can stay alive is to act like one of the butterflies in his collection. On the book's first page he says, "Seeing her always made me feel like I was catching a rarity," and he calls her, "A Pale Clouded Yellow," in the next sentence. His collection sets the bounds of his moral perspective. Not only Miranda, but all women are as butterflies to him. He says of a prostitute, "She was worn, common. Like a specimen you'd turn away from, out collecting." His sexual abnormality shows through in his preference for a variety of butterfly called *aberration*. And, in line with his infantilism, the sight of an imago makes him feel destructive. After Miranda dies he says, "I think we are just insects, we live a bit and then die and that's the lot." Her humanity has no place in his dead insect-world; rather than extending any freedom to her—even the freedom of a living insect—he kills her.

His reducing her to an object has political import. As Fowles says in *The Aristos,* any freedom must respect other freedoms: "All denigration of the rights to choose what shall make one happy . . . is fundamentally totalitarian." Clegg does not let Miranda choose her life, let alone her pleasures. As the following passage shows, his severing her from the outside world constitutes the absolute censorship of the fascist state:

> I never let her see papers. I never let her have a radio or television. It happened one day before ever she came I was reading a book called **Secrets of the Gestapo** . . . and how one of the first things to put up with if you were a prisoner was the not knowing what was going on outside the prison. I mean they didn't let the prisoners know anything, they didn't even let them talk to each other, so they were cut off from their old world. And that broke them down. Of course, I didn't want to break her down as the Gestapo wanted to break their prisoners down. But I thought it would be better if she was cut off from the outside world, she'd have to think about me more. So in spite of many attempts on her part to make me get her the papers and a radio I wouldn't let her have them. The first days I didn't want her to read about all the police were doing, and so on, because it would have only upset her. It was a kindness, as you might say.

The only time she looks at his butterfly collection, she reproves him, "You don't even share it. Who sees these? You're like a miser, you hoard up all the beauty in these drawers." *The Aristos* insists several times that existence is countersupporting and that human values come from counter-tension. By denying Miranda force, Clegg denies the polarity needed for normal life. The gerundive form of Latin *miror, miranda,* (that is, she who ought to be looked at), points up this denial etymologically. His rejection of interchange and shareability spells out the deathliness of his miniDictatorship. His will has created a closed circle that nothing human can pierce. He has declared himself the only sentient being in his perfect state. Because he has everything, need does not exist; because he is asocial, his realm has no society and no politics. His will is absolute; his end is his beginning. Miranda's first moments as his prisoner resemble her last; she is lying on a cot, her breathing congested. Inevitably, Clegg looks for another girl to take her place after she dies. "Another M!" he notes when he learns that Miranda's replacement has the name of Marian. Yet the differences between the two girls are as sharp as those between the white magic of *The Tempest* and the sullenness of *Measure for Measure,* where Marian of the moated grange appears. A shop assistant at Woolworth's, Marian is less resourceful than Miranda, less able to teach Clegg, and less suited to a prisoner's life. Though the novel ends before Marian's kidnapping, she will die several weeks before the two months the more adaptable Miranda kept alive.

Their differences notwithstanding, the two girls die cruel, wasteful deaths; totalitariansim does not respect human difference or individuality. Its success, in fact, depends on the eradication of differences. It cannot tolerate individuality. No one-party state can survive if it permits its aims and methods to be questioned. Miranda falls victim to the same controls exercised by the police state.

Power is a subject Fowles writes about with personal authority. Not only did he collect butterflies as a boy, but he also served as a Marine lieutenant and before that as both cricket captain and prefect, or head boy, at school. Power implies a master-slave relationship. In a *New York Times Book Review* interview, he discusses the evils of power; among them, it should be noted, is the tendency power has to recoil upon and corrode the powerful:

> Being head boy was a weird experience. You had total power over 800 other boys; you were totally responsible for discipline and

punishment. I spent my eighteenth year holding court, really. I'd have twenty boys before me every morning, who you were both prosecutor and judge of . . . and executioner, of course. I suppose I used to beat on average three or four boys a day. [5]

Arrogating to himself the roles of jailer, judge, and executioner seals all possible outlets of negotiation for Clegg. He epitomizes noncommunication. Soon after he moves into his house, he disconnects the phone, locks all gates and doors, and rudely dismisses the local vicar. Before he captured Miranda, he had wanted to send her two £ 5 notes anonymously but did not. After the capture, besides denying her access to radio, television, and the newspapers, he refuses to let her parents know she is still alive; he lies to her about sending a check for £ 100 to the Council for Nuclear Disarmament; he fails at sex. Where he never falters, though, is in the routine of locking and unlocking the doors of Miranda's cell during his visits. He even bolts her in after her death. Anything that puts barriers between people comes easily to him. The following quotation describes him sitting alone and reading about her disappearance in the newspapers:

I . . . read all the papers said. It gave me a feeling of power, I don't know why. All those people searching and me knowing the answer. When I drove on I decided definitely I'd say nothing to her.

Clegg's power over Miranda is so total that it inhibits nature. Besides removing the bracing countertension of social relations, it reorders space and time. It deprives Miranda of fresh air and sunshine, essential to all growing things. Ironically, this power defeats Clegg's pleasure; as has been said, his freedom and general well-being decline inversely with his growing power. Power loosens his control of the realities of his life.

Based on selfishness rather than sharing, tyranny is the

most rigid, closed-ended creed of all. A remark in *The Aristos* explains tyranny's limits in words appropriate to Clegg:

> [The tyrant] is enslaved by his own enslaving, tyrannized by his own tyranny. He is not free to act as he wishes because what he wishes is determined, and generally very narrowly, by the demands of maintaining tyranny.

Contrary to his aims, the police-state Clegg sets up by taking away Miranda's rights hampers him, the tyrant, more than her. Because she resists him she must be put down. As a result he denies himself a living source of human values. Rather than dealing openly with her he lies, and he either changes the subject or walks away when she raises the question of her freedom. All emergencies involving her health bring the same response—inaction; if the emergency is not faked, he reasons, then it will either right itself or, past help, kill Miranda in spite of his efforts to keep her alive. He cannot admit any contingencies besides those imposed by holding her prisoner. This is the gangster outlook of modern fascism. In that he destroys her rather than revising his credo, he is much more of a prisoner than she:

> What she never understood was that with me it was having. Having her was enough. Nothing needed doing. I just wanted to have her.

> I lived from day to day, really. I mean there was no plan. I just waited. I even half expected the police to come. I had a horrible dream one night when they came and I had to kill her before they came in the room . . . . I woke up in a sweat, that was the first time I ever dreamed of killing anyone.

The absence of civilized checks and restraints turns the nightmare into fact. Once again, this denial of process between Miranda and Clegg makes their life together a closed circle. Nothing new can come from their association; no stale value can be refreshed. Clegg's sexual failure is a logical corollary of his death-drift. A natural act shared by people, sex is beyond him. He can communicate neither intellectually nor physically. Inaction and violence are the only two responses open to him. As has been said, *The Collector* has a severe logic. Miranda's humanity keeps flaring out in search of warm contacts. Since these outbursts oppose Clegg's wishes, he can only kill her.

A sure sign of his failure is his disregard of chance or hazard. Hazard, Fowles keeps insisting, defines freedom. If intelligence can be called the ability to handle the unforeseen, then hazard hones the intelligence. In his thick, dull way, Clegg never adapts to the needs created by hazard. He is immobilized by the unexpected and accidental. Like any other despot, he wants everything predictable, and he will use force and lies to guard the frontiers of predictability. Ironically, Miranda has always legislated for herself; she is airy, buoyant, sparkling. He has never been self-acting. He says that capturing her is "the first wicked think I've ever done." But it is also the first thing of *any* kind he has done. As soon as he and Miranda meet and reverse their roles of agent and acted-upon, they are done for. Although the irony escapes him, the hazard situation that made him rich also brought Miranda to him. But by converting his luck to destruction, he misuses luck. Miranda is only the first in a series. The chance appearance of a policeman outside the doctor's home where Clegg goes to get help for Miranda clinches the hazard theme. Besides deepening Clegg's failure, the scene, coming at the end, balances his winning the lottery at the outset. Both ends of the book feature hazard. His fantasy cannot pad the impact that hazard makes on his life.

Another impact the novel delivers comes from the idea that every life is redeemable. Clegg is weak, but not stupid;

unimaginative, but not slipshod. He prepares for Miranda's arrival with amazing cunning—building the door of her cell to look like a bookcase, setting up a burglar-alarm system, installing a special incinerator to burn her rubbish, sleeping in her room to check the air supply, buying aluminum cutlery and plastic dishes. Nor is he tasteless or aesthetically blind. His attraction to Miranda bears out his sense of beauty. And while she despises him, her view of him relative to herself does vary. She admits, "He really had a sort of dignity," and on the next page she adds, "He had more dignity than I did then and I felt small, mean." The pure primitive contact of sex with him excites her. Also, though he has little distinction, he is memorable. She recognizes him from the Town Hall Annexe where he worked, and she recalls his winning a great sum in the football pools. There is much more to him than mechanical efficiency. His occasional oversights, like carelessly leaving his odd-jobs axe where she can lay hands on it, show that he is human. Were he completely mechanized, he would overlook nothing.

Yet he throws away his gift for organization and compassion. A self-declared existentialist, Fowles claims that what man does with his natural endowments counts more than the endowments themselves. Any potential must be translated into performance before it has value. Clegg squanders his potential because he cannot rise above his mania for collecting. The book's title encompasses him; to blot out the collector in him would leave nothing. His possessions possess him. A 1970 statement by Fowles points out the totalitarian dangers of collecting: "Any one who still collects (*i.e.,* kills) some field of living life just for pleasure and vanity has all the makings of a concentration-camp commandant." Then Fowles calls collecting "a narcissistic and parasitical" hobby.[6] Killing, collecting, and exercising power are continuous and interchangeable. A dead butterfly cannot breed; it leaves no progeny to delight or instruct nature lovers; once killed and mounted, it is denied the right to live. Maurice Conchis says that collecting kills the moral instinct; an art collector in *The Magus* owns "a withered, dusty sea cucumber," said to be the Holy Member. That the man dies at the same time his collection burns proves that collectors can only live among dead things. Like fascist politics, collecting thrives on stasis. An object in a collector's hoard usually stays there. Often, nobody but the collector sees it. The joy of collecting, in fact, springs largely from not sharing. Like a miser, the collector gets less pleasure from owning an object than from knowing that others do not own it. In the meantime, the object loses its color and force; it becomes the reverse of a mystery.

The menace of collecting cannot be overstated. By destroying dialogue, collecting rules out the hope of making moral distinctions and deciding degrees of freedom. It becomes its own end ("Having her was enough. Nothing needed doing. I just wanted to have her."). It degrades man in all but the material sense. Quality gets subordinated to quantity. Competing for bulk or numbers, collectors amass ever larger collections. They kill more life; everything becomes an object. Clegg shows that the consumer-industrial state must give way to the university state. If pleasure remains a function of having ("the monetization of pleasure"), goods designed to have a short life drive out ones made to last. The death of craftsmanship undermines tradition. Artifacts do not survive a generation; aesthetic standards disappear; relationships grow interchangeable. Clegg and his butterfly collection pollute British culture. He spoils his "lovely old house" with hideous furnishings and decorations. "A house as old as this has a soul," Miranda tells him, revolted by the house's tacky appointments: "Ghastly color-clashes, mix-up of furniture styles, bits of suburban fuss, phoney antiques, awful brass ornaments. And the pictures!

You wouldn't believe . . . the awfulness of the pictures." The house, scheduled by The Ancient Monuments Commission, was built in 1621; local legend says that the dank bin where Clegg stows Miranda is a secret Roman Catholic chapel. By shutting a scheduled house and turning its chapel into a prison, Clegg defiles tradition. (But English tradition is already in danger; with young people like Clegg and the agent who sells him his house enjoying power without responsibility, middle-aged people fighting to keep young, and the under-mining of craftsmanship by the camera, links with the past have weakened.)

But why should he worry about wrecking tradition? What has tradition done for him to make him want to protect it? He has never owned property nor learned a skill. He even works in an annex. His ignorance of due process leads him to take what he wants. Everything tallies. Clegg has not learned respect for the law because the law did not respect *him* enough to educate him properly. His problem is universal; social equality and justice cannot come from material possessions. What is needed above all is educational reform. Clegg belongs in a classroom or hospital, not a prison.

II

The encounter of Miranda and Clegg spells out this need. Being one of the Few does not confer superiority so much as the responsibility to teach and help the Many. Her physical death and his moral death express the difficulty of making good the responsibility. Miranda voices Fowles's humanistic objections as well as his passion for educational reform. She probably carries her narrative burden less well than Clegg, though. Readers have complained that Fowles's liberal-humanist conception of her makes her merely a literary man's model of an ideal girl. The following extract from her diary, though, describes her as more of a sociology major on the rampage than a humanities student:

> I hate the uneducated and the ignorant. I hate the pompous and the phoney. I hate the jealous and resentful. I hate the crabbed and the mean and the petty. I hate all ordinary dull little people who aren't ashamed of being dull and little. I hate . . . the New People, the new-class people with their cars and their money and their tellies and their stupid vulgarities and their stupid crawling imitation of the bourgeoisie.

The declaration has the shrillness of a platform manifesto. Silly and overcharged Miranda is. But her melodrama comes from a surplus of youthful moral passion. Her gropings are honest and forceful. Had she lived, she would have outgrown her romantic posturing and become somebody exceptional, perhaps even an evolutionary force. In 1965 Fowles called her "an existentialist heroine": "She's groping for her authenticity. Her tragedy is that she will never live to achieve it. Her triumph is that one day she would have done so."[7]

She is like Shakespeare's Miranda in *The Tempest,* with her beauty, innocence, hope, moral idealism, and rage for experience. A brave new world shimmers before her that she hungers to confront. She is filled with expectation; her head brims with pictures; her heart brims with principles. Though this potential good is snuffed out by the actuality of Clegg's evil, she does win a major battle. Clegg stoops to lies, evasiveness, and violence, but she maintains dignity by refusing to respond in kind. She is kidnapped to begin with because of her compassion. She pities the dog that Clegg pretends he ran over, and when she looks in his van he chloroforms her. The only advantages he enjoys over her are his superior physical strength and his money; and money, as it is in D.H. Lawrence, is a form of violence.

A major theme in the book is the battle between spirit and dull, sluggish matter. The winner here is Miranda, and though its moral lesson escapes Clegg, her victory constitutes a major triumph. Only a clear, strong spirit could wrest gains from her situation. Her captivity makes incredible demands on her. Clegg will give her anything but freedom; at the same time, his submissiveness puts her in charge of everything except her being. He gives her nothing human to work with. He and she are remote without enjoying any of the dignity and reserve of remoteness; they are extremely close but not intimate. By demanding nothing but her extended captivity, he makes her ordeal one of terror and boredom, claustrophobia and endless blankness. Counterweighting her cramped cell is a vague grey stretch of time. Yet, to her credit, she uses this time well, raising her inner life above her physical bondage. First, she maintains her high standards. Though she does act badly on occasion, she never sinks to Clegg's level. That her body breaks before her mind celebrates her steely creativity. This tragic victory shows most clearly in the scene where she hits Clegg with an axe. Her humanity outweighs her instinct for survival. She never wanted to kill him. But by not following her temporary advantage, she does not knock him out either. Violence is simply not her way. Though Clegg deserves to be axed, she repents her outburst the next morning by apologizing and then dressing his wound.

Fowles neither resolves nor dissolves moral complexities. Miranda's death does not smoothe the spirit-matter dualism. In fact, it makes us ask whether we *should* fight to preserve what we love and live by. Miranda's failure to knock Clegg unconscious leads to her own death as well as to a number of other deaths. Life makes strange demands. Clegg has created an airless, bloodless realm whose laws deny good conduct. He has created this unnatural order without consulting Miranda. By adopting his measures to defend herself, she outrages her principles. But moral principle only prolongs the terror she lives under. Her life is at stake. And to gainsay life is to gainsay all. If she defends herself immorrally, her range of choice has shrunk so far that the only alternative is death. Miranda sticks by her principles and dies.

But are principles worth dying for? Fowles's dislike of the pat answer and his fascination for the region of "what might have been" lead him to sidestep the question in favor of portraying Miranda as an existential heroine-in-the-making. It has been seen how she uses her time well and keeps her moral standards high. Even more remarkable than this tenacity is the internal growth and strength that made it possible. She develops in spite of her handicaps, reaching the point where she can say, "I am beginning to understand life much better than most people of my age." Though hampered, she calls herself lucky. Avoiding self-pity, she redecorates her cell. She evolves a new theory of painting and later puts the theory into practice. Seeing her mother clearly for the first time, she comes to know and love her. Even her growing atheism figures in the victory she gains over the drab clay of her jailer. She learns that she has only herself to rely on. She learns to temper her actionism: "I've always tried to happen to life; but it's time I let life happen to me." This quietism brings self-knowledge. showing her the difference between solitude and loneliness. Solitude gives her the ballast and control to refurbish her moral vision and, in the process, convert Clegg's dullness into a healthy negative influence.

She reaffirms in her heart the primacy of commitment. The commitment she rethinks most carefully is the one she shares with George Paston, or G.P., a London artist of about forty who never appears materially in the book. By ordinary standards, Paston has failed; ordinary standards also make him an unlikely lover for Miranda. Twice her age, physically ugly, and shorter than Miranda, he seems to have little to offer her. His paintings have not earned him fame or money; his teen-aged sons are ashamed of him; he keeps having empty sexual affairs. Yet he has remained free, following his aesthetic lights, and his freedom gives him a suddenness and integrity unique in Miranda's life. "He always makes *me* think," she says of him. "That's the big thing. He makes me question myself." The aliveness of their relationships defies labels. She sees him as "suddenly much, much older than me"; three pages later, she says, "suddenly he seemed much younger than me." He calls her "the daughter I'd like to have," but then says, "Perhaps morally I'm younger even then you are." Their relationship, with its Oedipal tinge, is flawed, tainted, and, because they have never had sex, also untested. They are rarely alone. Most of their meetings happen by chance and end prematurely. They get little happiness from each other.

This abrasiveness denotes life. Miranda cannot explain her feelings for him: "I can't explain it. There isn't a word for it." What she does call him is "the most important person I have ever met." Unlike Clegg, he succeeds with her because he rises above proofs and tangible facts. Eclipsing the letter of the law, he has the faith and independence to accept hazard. Miranda writes of him in successive diary entries:

> If he really loved me he couldn't send me away.
> If he really loved me he would have sent me away.

A final sign of his creative influence on her is her summoning him, not Clegg, in her last moments of consciousness. Yet her Prospero can only steel her for her ordeal; he cannot release her from it. The Calibanity of Clegg exacts strict obedience to his commodity fetish. To his anguished frame of mind, his motives have a metaphysical necessity.

The religious theme of *The Collector* is hinted at by the supposition that Miranda is being held prisoner in an old priest's chapel. The date of the house, 1621, puts the theme in a severe context: the Pilgrims landed at Plymouth Rock in 1620, and the Puritans set up their American commonwealth in 1629. Clegg's family is also nonconformist. The harshness of their low-church outlook, which includes the loveless notion of original sin, explains much of Clegg's conduct. Clegg plays God with Miranda. The only freedom she has is the freedom he gives her. Instead of treating her as a child of God, he makes her an idea in his mind. She only exists when he thinks of her. In a hideous parallel to Berkeleian idealism, he has her at his mercy. Her being is enclosed by his. Her survival depends wholly on him:

> What happens if he has a crash? A stroke. Anything. I die.
> I couldn't get out. All I did the day before yesterday was to prove it.

Berkeley is not the only philosopher who illuminates the religious aspects of Miranda's ordeal. The religious existentialists, Gabriel Marcel and Martin Buber, also come into play. Buber's *I and Thou* interprets life as a dialogue between active, perceiving subjects. The Thou is no It; and I-It encounter is no exchange or dialogue at all. Marcel has a good corollary to Buber's argument in his "participation" philosophy. To accept the reality of other people is to declare belief in God; it reflects faith in God's ability to people the world with sentient beings. Instead of lying inert and flat, the world hums with opportunities for pleasure and proft. Yet Clegg's slavishness bars him from this vitality. All of Miranda's attempts to make him human divide her from him, sinking him deeper in the false security of his collection.

It has been seen how collecting inhibits process. As a harsh God who gives and takes away life, Clegg violates natural and supernatural law. He denies Miranda many of the necessities of animal, let alone, human survival. The sternest Puritanism offers more scope and promise than he gives her,

("Perhaps I was overstrict, I erred on the strict side"). Like other Christian faiths, Calvinism distinguishes between God and man; were God and man the same, Christ would not have come to earth. But Christ did visit man as an interceder, and His spirit survives as the Holy Ghost, or love. Though we do not deserve divine favor, God's grace, the fount of all love, keeps some of us out of hell. We are not all damned, says Protestant fundamentalism; there is hope for a few. But hope does not even exist marginally in *The Collector*. Nothing like the Holy Ghost joins Miranda to the graceless Clegg. He is without heart. He buys her a heart-shaped necklace in sapphires and diamonds, and, while she has it on, hears her say, "We don't have the same sort of heart." Elsewhere she says, referring to the fiction he uses to kidnap her, "That story about the dog. He uses my heart. Then turns and tramples on it." This heartlessness sharpens the Christian parallel. God, foreseeing the crucifixion, sent Christ to earth because the divine attribute of perfection rules out suffering. Clegg has no more ability to suffer than the God of Christianity; a pitiless iron law grips him with all the strength of a metaphysical necessity. But he lacks God's compassion and wisdom. He also lacks the heart to inspire the devotion Christ demanded from his followers. His violation of Miranda's nature and his denial of renewability make him a poor God-surrogate. The divine power he arrogates to himself, having no natural or supernatural sanction, can only lead to death.

This down-dragging inertia, his underground dungeon, and his sense of injured merit all suggest Satan. Clegg sins against the Holy Ghost, and his moral darkness tallies with an affinity for the dark. Darkness is his natural milieu. He prowls around London's parks in the dark, he develops his fetishist pictures in his dark room, and he admits that he could not have captured Miranda in clear weather. But there is nothing flashy about his evil. A mousy, fawning Satan, he has no imagination or verbal wit. His unworldliness is the demonic principle, not sophistication. The innocence-experience dualism does not apply in *The Collector*. The experience of sin need not taint or maim; more often, innocence is what destroys. Maleducation and "the horrid timid genteel in-between class" whose values he has inherited lead him to lie, degrade, and finally kill. His frequent blushes recall Satan's redness. And his cringing, run-down evil is Satanic in a way continuous with his social class, where the New People have more money and power than they can use responsibly.

But what of Miranda's blushes? And why does Fowles have her say that her heart differs from Clegg's while she has on the heart-shaped necklace he gives her? Although he does trample her heart, he only puts on the necklace because she asks him to; the pendent necklace, moreover, dips below her throat to her breastbone and heart. Fowles's moral preference for Miranda is not as thoroughgoing as it appears. A comment in the 1970 version of *The Aristos* deepens the complexity. Fowles describes Clegg as a victim of forces beyond his control, and he catalogues Miranda's negative qualities:

> I tried to show that his evil was largely, perhaps wholly, the result of a bad education, a mean environment, being orphaned: all factors over which he had no control. In short, I tried to establish the virtual **innocence** of the Many. Miranda . . . had very little more control than Clegg over what she was: she had well-to-do parents, good educational opportunity, inherited aptitude and intelligence. That does not mean that she was perfect. Far from it—she was arrogant in her ideas, a prig, a liberal-humanist snob.

Like this comment, Fowles's insistence that we all share traits of the Few and Many and William Wyler's billing of the film version of *The Collector* as "almost a love story" both realign moral issues in the novel. So does the following statement by Thomas Churchill in *Critique*: "The boy and the girl are not really much different . . . they might find a way if they worked at it hard enough."[8] The moral picture has taken on an unexpected tint. Churchill's apparently far-fetched statement reminds us of the many similarities between Clegg and Miranda. They both blush often; he has a job in the neighborhood where she lives; then they inhabit the same house; each has an alcoholic mother; each refers to people by initial rather than name. She notes that his mad eyes are grey, but Grey is also her last name. Clegg's fantasy that he can make her love him by keeping her prisoner is wild, but wild too are many of her ideas about art, marriage, and social justice. In fact, she has ten wild ideas in her head for every one of his. As repulsive as he is, she makes sexual overtures to him, and she admits in her diary, "There is a sort of relationship between us." She also admits, "I am his madness." By attracting what destroys her, must she share his guilt? She has the moral strength to resist evil deeds. He sins involuntarily. His inability to stop abducting and killing girls makes him more pathetic than she.

The moral ambiguities lengthen. Fowles even obscures pronoun references in her diary to keep the reader from knowing whether she is talking about Clegg or George Paston. The tremendous human distance between the two men matches the distance in outlook dividing Miranda from Clegg. Fowles's ironical dovetailings do more than just point out the characters' common humanity. They also turn his drama beyond causality and bend his indirect questions about guilt and responsibility to the unchartered depths of primitive experience.

III

The device of the alternating diaries captures the major irony of the book—the difference between Clegg's view of the abduction and Miranda's. The diaries convey the minds of the characters, so that the reader knows more about their common situation than either of them does. Motives, private histories, and strategies of each character come into view. Clegg's sexual impotence and Miranda's carefully planned attempt to dig her way out of the dungeon, coming as diary or memoir entries, give the reader more information about the abduction than either character alone has. Specifically, Miranda's chance for freedom shrinks progressively with our growing knowledge of Clegg. He will resort to any oversight, distortion, or lie to justify holding Miranda prisoner. So dogged is he in his rectitude that when the first part ends, nearly halfway into the book, his confession hurls the reader into Part Two, which is Miranda's diary; his confession reads:

> What I am trying to say is that it all came unexpected. I know what I did next day was a mistake, but up to that day I thought I was acting for the best and within my rights.

While Clegg's memoir describes his moral darkness, it also humanizes him. The effortless drive and fluency of the memoir, by giving a sustained private view, commits us to him imaginatively. This intimate self-disclosure is necessary, for a third-person narrative about someone as repellent as Clegg would set so much distance between him and us that he would come to us as a caricature or a monster. The memoir's mad, twisted logic, flat, colorless voice, and autobiographical data cohere as a self-portrait. Certain recurring attitudes deepen his madness. There is the withering disclosure voiced as a vague afterthought: Sexual magnetism is "some crude animal thing I was born without. (And I'm glad I was, if more people were like me, in my opinion, the world would be better.)": "I think people like Mabel [his invalid cousin] should be put out painlessly, but that's beside the point." There is also the protest of innocence, like his disclaiming responsibility for

Miranda's death: "I didn't know what I was doing half the time": "I wanted her to be better by then, so I suppose I was seeing things." Sometimes he will use a seedy euphemism to prettify a vile act. Contrary to intention, these euphemisms emphasize his self-deceit, his failure to detach himself from social class, and his indifference to Miranda's pain. When he makes her pose naked for photographs, he ties her up and gags her. Then he says he "got her garments off." And just before he buries her, he calls her "the deceased." Our spinal fluid turns to ice.

Fowles interposes Miranda's diary (Part Two) after she catches cold but before her last illness. Part Two goes up to the time of her delirium; there is no time lag between the end of Part One, the end of Part Two, and the start of Part Three, where Clegg's voice takes over again. The stylistic differences between the two accounts are jolting. Clegg's style is blunt, flat, and conservative. His shrunken, timorous mind prefers facts to speculation and interpretation. Miranda's style bespeaks her artistic, outgoing nature. It sparkles with color and sound. She uses language like daubs of paint on a sketchpad. Her lyrical, loose-jointed sentences hold together by free association; she sometimes uses one-word paragraphs; whereas Clegg abides slavishly by grammatical rules, her rippling, imagistic prose abounds in sentence fragments. A painter by preference and training, she adapts well to the medium of words. So eager is she to try new modes that she writes part of the diary as a play with dialogue and stage directions.

Though her diary repeats some of the events Clegg related, it cannot be faulted for repetitiousness. The diary is not informational in thrust; its main job is to describe the staleness of prison life and also her creative responses to her enslavement. Clegg has not imprisoned her mind along with her body. He says, "It was like we were the only two people in the world." But her diary proves him wrong. She spends much time discussing George Paston, or G.P., whereas Clegg discusses only her. The entries devoted to G.P. explain that she has a life Clegg cannot touch; her world is not limited to him as his is to her. Instead of endearing her to him, her enslavement has the reverse effect of heightening her awareness of Paston. The entries dealing with Clegg are mostly short, choppy, and factual; those on Paston are more speculative, expansive, and expressive of her personality. Sometimes an entry, like the one of 26 October, will start out discussing Clegg but will end by talking about Paston.

As with Clegg, whose terror sharpens by being couched in a blunt, matter-of-fact idiom, Miranda's literary style gauges her personality, her values, and her ability to adapt to chance. The stylistic inventiveness and control of *The Collector* fuel the novel's theme. *The Collector* is not a perfect novel. The symbolism at the end thickens and obtrudes: Clegg denies three pleas from Miranda for a doctor; her last words are, "I forgive you"; he buries her under an apple tree. Offsetting these blemishes is a marvelous narrative gift. No simplistic diversion, *The Collector* is a brilliant first novel. It features two people who have nothing in common and nothing to say to each other. The end of the book finds them more apart than ever. Yet the book overcomes these plot handicaps to strike roots in postwar British society and to flower in all time. Only an artist could have written it.

NOTES TO CHAPTER 2

1. Newquist, pp. 223, 222.
2. Ibid., p. 219.
3. Ibid., pp. 218, 225.
4. John Fowles, "In Paradise," *Transatlantic Review* 14 (Autumn 1963): 9.
5. Boston, p. 2.
6. Fowles, "Weeds, Bugs, Americans," p. 99.

7. Newquist, p. 225.

8. Thomas Churchill, "Waterhouse, Storey, and Fowles: Which Way out of the Room," *Critique* 10 [n.d.]: 82.

3
Beings and Becomings, Icons and Incidents

Fowles's brilliance reasserts itself in *The Magus* with increased surge. Instead of dealing with just two characters within a single setting, he ranges freely over Western Europe, uses many characters, and rehearses ideas from history, psychology, and philosophy. Its sustained power, verve, and range of reference make *The Magus* a booming, colorful book. Guy Davenport calls it "one of the most exciting and wildly rich novels of our time"; Mudrick praises it as "shrewd and lively, brilliantly visualized, continuously provoking and entertaining." Richard Stolley refers warmly to "the sheer mind-rocking richness of the prose," and Brian Moore commends both the genuineness of Fowles's narrative gift and his fine manipulation of suspense.[1] Moore's commendation has merit. For suspense does promote much of the book's excitement. The screws keep tightening on Nicholas Urfe, the main character and narrator, as Fowles, who mentions James's *Turn of the Screw,* strips him of dignity, reason, and hope. We wonder at Urfe's ability to take punishment. Then the novel reshapes itself as a detective story; the battered Urfe takes a more active role, and Fowles brings in a chase, several clues, a mystery to solve, and a chain of bewildering appearances and disappearances. Moore is not alone in noticing the novel's resemblance to crime fiction. W.W. Robson calls *The Magus* a thriller, and Mudrick, alluding to the intellectual challenge posed by most crime fiction, says,

"*The Magus* may well be . . . one of the best 'mystery stories' ever written . . . an incitement to consciousness."[2]

But the book's intellectual drive does not dissolve in the deductive challenge of solving a crime. *The Magus* reveals Fowles at his most mobile, limber, and learned. Besides qualifying as detective fiction, it studies war, surveys modern European history, and discusses manners and morals, especially as they relate to sexual love. Its emphasis on intangibles like feeling, rather than cause-and-effect materialism, puts the novel in a literary tradition more French than English. Among other things, *The Magus* is a novel of sensibility. It does not study social institutions, and it does not record the impact of society upon the individual. Instead, Fowles probes inward. His working premise, as usual, is that all knowledge is self-knowledge; though he sees society as a complex web of relationships, his real interest is prime being. Alison Kelly tells Urfe, the first time they meet, "Now let's talk about what we really are," and says later to him, "I know what you are." Urfe is advised, "Marry her [Alison] and have a family and learn to be what you really are," and then admonished, "I can't understand any man not realizing what she was underneath." Fowles uses a great deal of formal learning to dig into this core of selfhood. He refers freely to notable writers and painters; his familiarity with music includes Arbeau, Frescobaldi, and Froberger; his knowledge of ceramics extends to rhytons, kylixes, and amphoras; his characters speak Latin, Italian, Spanish, French, German, Norwegian, English, and both classical and demotic Greek. The many references in these languages to mythology, the arts, and cultural history have made the book, in the eyes of several critics, a survey course in Western civilization.

And like any other good course, *The Magus* does not leave the reader, or student, where it finds him. It sends him into himself, fusing a Jamesian attention to form—which requires that everything be integrated, balanced, and rele-vant—with the expansiveness of earlier Victorian fiction. Theme and action go together. *The Magus* carries its moral in its action; no overdocumentation, cultural chic, or surface newsiness weakens the tie joining the story, plot, and theme. Aesthetically, the book is anachronistic, both bypassing the middle-class domestic realism of Amis, Wain, and Angus Wilson and giving no inside view of the English working class, like Sillitoe and David Storey. *The Magus* has important similarities with the exotic romance, its poetic qualities surpassing those of even *The Alexandria Quartet.* No dry polemic, it is a very physical book, driving into the nerves and sinews. Another feature it shares with good poetry is its ability to blur frontiers between illusion and reality and between physical and mental experience. It does not pretend to know where mind ends and body begins. Like *Ulysses,* it is analytic and inventive, urbane and earthy, theoretical and therapeutic all at once. It roars with technical effects; its brilliance dazzles. Yet its strong, pure voice never slides into demented extravaganza. Fowles's vivid showmanship has a place for the tentative and the oblique. Classicist and modernist, he does not look for ways to impose his personality; his sound judgment keeps him from trying to do more than instruct and entertain; his sense of the ridiculous keeps him from becoming pompous, uncouth, or long-winded.

Still, the performance of *The Magus*—its learning, its granite ambitiousness, its virtuosity—overrides everything else. Several discerning readers have complained that it never digests the great raw chunks of experience it takes into its bloodstream. Joyce Carol Oates called it "confused in its cunning"; Angus Wilson, in a review entitled "Fowles's Foul Fantasy," called it "overingenious" and badly cluttered. Brian Moore's review, "Too Much Hocus in the Pocus," attacked Fowles's Magus-figure as "a mixture of Somerset Maugham and Dr. Fu Manchu." More recently (1970),

Bernard Bergonzi charged the book with self-indulgence and disunity: "The whole novel is not much more than a highly inventive series of fantastic or cruel episodes. . . .The novel is vitiated by its basic pointlessness, its inability to relate to anything except itself." [3]

These attacks cannot be disregarded. But the congestion that they all allude to exists only marginally, if at all. *The Magus* needs its plenitude of data to carry forward its theme, as a contrast with *The Collector* will show. *The Collector* stayed close to reality, uncovering the dark, deadly cruelty of the commonplace. It explored the related issues of guilt, innocence, and responsibility, by describing the evil of banality. Its main figure, Frederick Clegg, deepened the exploration with his destructive innocence. Though innocent, too, Urfe is a destructive, irresponsible cosmopolite—he is an Oxford graduate, he knows languages, writes poetry, has had a number of love affairs, and has also lived and worked outside England. His background, his nature, and his openness to change call for a more sophisticated technique than that of *The Collector*. Fowles also creates a stunning double remove by interposing several years between Urfe's memoir and the events it recounts. The lapse of years extends the scope of the Godgame. It allows Urfe to present a younger version of himself, which he does without condescension or special pleading. Next, the lapse between the 1953 setting and 1965 publication date of *The Magus* puts the book in what Henry James called "the visitable past." 1953 was still familiar territory to a 1965 reader; Fowles compels an extra measure of reader involvement. Also, the twelve-year interval removed the problem of distinguishing surface from inner reality. This distinction—between surface dash and the truths people live by—cannot be made in one's own age. Nor can social satire gain the authority of historical perspective in a narrative set in the present.

The sharp focus and historical thrust afforded by the 1953 time-setting gain voice in the book's out-of-balance first sentence: "I was born in 1927, the only child of middle-class parents, both English, and themselves born in the grotesquely elongated shadow, which they never rose sufficiently above history to leave, of that monstrous dwarf Queen Victoria." In this teasing invocation of the novel's epical theme lies extravagance alongside simplicity. Most of the sentence is a long adjectival clause. What starts as a simple declarative statement of fact ends as a chain of right-branching phrases and clauses that go further and further from the subject and main verb. This busy, ungainly syntax echoes the situation of Tom Jones and his literary offspring, who scramble a great deal but accomplish very little. *The Magus* belongs in the tradition of English fiction called *comical-epical* and associated with Fielding and, sometimes, Joyce. Like Tom Jones and Leopold Bloom, Nicholas Urfe wastes effort, fails to recoup losses caused by his own stupidity, and shows little moral improvement after a long moral ordeal. In all three cases, however, this improvement is real. Furthermore, it rests on the ability to understand a few simple truths. The elaborate machinery of *The Magus* describes the attainment of this wisdom as a hard struggle for those born without it; in order to make an impact, truths must be lived, not imposed or explained. Everything useful is situational, relative, and intensely personal. What truth is, then, and what it means to Urfe will make more sense when built dramatically into his situation.

I

Penelope Mortimer finds this situation leaden and static: Urfe for her is "the professional antihero—not fascinating, but not dull either; not tremendously interesting, but not altogether boring; not really attractive, but not actively repellent." [4] Not so middling as Miss Mortimer says, Urfe embodies counterstresses that do not offset so much as resonate with each other. Fowles does not want a one-to-one stalemate. Thus transcendental and descendental qualities mix in Urfe. Nick, which he is sometimes called, is the name of the devil; yet he is once called Saint Nicholas, and he does emerge more than once as a bringer of gifts. His last name, with its phonetic resemblance to earth, reminds us that he is as clayish and base as Frederick Clegg. This baseness, though, is somewhat offset by his love for poetry and the family legend that traces his descent to Honoré d'Urfé, author of *L'Astrée*, the famous seventeenth-century fictional meditation on love. But Urfe dishonors both his namesake and the tradition connected with him because he cannot love. As his initials suggest, he is a new, post-1945 man, distracted from love by the false gods of modern life.

Urfe's having no love to give causes most of his problems. A psychologist says of him, "The most significant feature of his life-style is negative: its lack of social content." The diagnosis is correct. At the book's outset, he is a jaded pseudosophisticate of twenty-five, his tour of military duty and a third-class Oxford degree both behind him. He has no job and feels strongly about nothing. The passive verb and negative qualifier in the novel's opening paragraph capture his inertia: "I was sent to a public school, I wasted two years doing my national service, I went to Oxford; and there I began to discover I was not the person I wanted to be." Sex is important to him, but in a depersonalized way; he has become as adept at ending affairs as at starting them. Not motivated by freedom, he simply fears the responsibility of a close sexual tie. But he cannot be indicted for self-deceit. A redeeming honesty he acquires at Oxford lets him face his failures directly:

Nothing could have been less poetic than my pseudo-aristocratic, seeing-through boredom with life . . . . I was too green to know that all cynicism masks a failure to cope—an impotence, in short . . . . The truth was that I was not a cynic by nature; only by revolt. I had got away from what I hated, but I hadn't found where I loved, and so I pretended there was nowhere to love.

His revolt is very 1950-ish. A parentless liberal-arts major in a commercial, science-haunted society, he lacks moorings. He travels a lot; he strikes defensive postures; he takes himself too seriously; he explains his personal setbacks by nostrums like the Bomb, the Age, and the Battle of the Sexes. Unable to judge things on their merits, he lacks the force to muster a real revolt. Like Osborne's Jimmy Porter in *Look Back in Anger,* he is a self-pitying rebel without a cause. The strongest influence on him, aside from his era, is his father, an irascible brigadier general who died while Urfe was at Oxford. The harsh discipline imposed both by "Blazer" Urfe's job and personality gives his son the need to rebel. What he resents in particular is male authority; unable to protest effectively, he compensates by preying sexually on young women. His failing, an inability to conduct a personal relationship, is patently male, as the following pronouncement by Maurice Conchis indicates. The dovetailing of maleness and war, it needs saying, includes the fact that Urfe's father was a career soldier:

That is the great distinction between the sexes. Men see objects, women see the relationship between objects . . . . I will tell you what war is. War is a psychosis caused by an inability to see relationships. Our relationship with our fellowmen.

Steepening this failure is the carpe diemism that rules our consumer society: effort must show some kind of profit, some gain. Rather than devoting time and energy to the prospect of building a friendship, it has become more expedient (and emotionally safer) to take from people, that is, to use them. Inevitably, the next step is to the collector's hoard of dead things: "When the whole philosophy of . . . [a consumer-industrial] society can be reduced to this: You owe yourself as much as you can get, whether it be in money, in status, in possessions, in enjoyments, or in experience, Can pleasure not become a duty?" (*The Aristos*). Urfe's pursuit of pleasure leads him to Alison Kelly, a young Australian he quickly subdues to his needs. He projects a view of her that he obtrudes between her reality and what he sees as duty to self. So, deciding that the actual pleasure she gives him is blocking a potentially greater pleasure, he gives her up. But after several months, he decides he wants her and nearly goes mad trying to win her back. This conduct is sentimental in the worst sense. The offered and the real bore him. That Alison is most real to him *in absentia* shows in his preference for the difficult and the remote. Here is where he wastes effort. Because most things in his society come with a price tag, he scorns the freely given. Like Citizen Charles Kane, he must go to great lengths to recover a prize he once had, undervalued, and lost.

To be more specific, Urfe meets Alison in London, where each has gone to find a new job and, though neither knows it, a new mystery. Urfe has just left a dull teaching job and an overheated love affair in the provinces; Alison wants a job as a flight attendant. "A kind of human oxymoron" who rules out ordinary value judgments, she tests his humanity. In order to acccept her, Urfe must first overcome his British class-prejudice of looking down on Australians as raw colonials. But razing class hurdles would not make his heart any more loving. His amorous exploits show that his fear of love does not include sex. He enjoys sex most, in fact, when unencumbered by love. And though he does not consciously thwart love, the love-sex dualism persists in his mind throughout.

Midway into the book, he and Alison make "not sex, but love; though sex would have been wiser."

Though mindful of Alison's deep, loving need for him, he leaves London to teach at the romantically named Lord Byron School on a Grecian island called Phraxos. Fowles's naming the school after Lord Byron touches on Urfe's self-image as a poet and a romantic exile. It also hits a parallel between Byron's rampant sexuality and Urfe's. Just as sex may have compensated for Byron's limp, so does it cloak a wound in Urfe. A society of shakers and movers prizes action, accumulation, and variety. Urfe, the self-styled social rebel, obeys his society's formula for success. He does not regret leaving Alison for the Lord Byron School and Greece. Only later does he admit mistaking his emotional dryness for freedom.

Also suggested by the Byronic parallel is a contrast between art and morality and between intellectual detachment and emotional involvement. Greece Urfe sees as an escape through art, calling it "a clean canvas, a site for myths." He compares his arrival in Greece to Alice's in Wonderland, and he even views Greece as Alison's love rival:

> What Alison was not to know—since I hardly realized it myself—was that I had been deceiving her with another woman . . . .The woman was Greece . . . . I got hold of all the books I could find on the country. It astounded me how little I knew about it. I read and read; and I was like a medieval king, I had fallen in love with the picture long before I saw the reality.
>
> I fell head over heels, totally and forever in love with the Greek landscape from the moment I arrived.

Greece whets his escapist tendency of forsaking the moral for the aesthetic sphere. A would-be poet, he reduces life to a literary game, particularly in times of stress; an artistic problem is easier to cope with than a human one. It gives wide berth to the things we live by; like any other abstraction, it can be shelved or even forgotten. Thus acting like a character in a novel or play eases many of the tensions in Urfe's life. Referring to this escapism, he mentions "this characteristically twentieth-century retreat from content into form, from meaning into appearance, from ethics into aesthetics." His teaching job in Greece, his poetry, and his suicidal impulses all thwart life. Life is to be lived, not written about, and it is best lived close to one's ancestral and cultural roots. Urfe chides himself for playing a role to impress an invisible observer—"a god like a novelist." Art holds reality away if we mistake it for a true rather than a metaphorical description. Urfe's many wrong turnings prove "the total inadequacy of the confused value judgments and pseudo-statements of art to equip man for his evolutionary role." Fowles has not lost his faith in evolution. But man evolves for him through chance, not art.

Urfe's punishment suits his crime. Gainsaying life in favor of art, he undergoes an extended ordeal by art. The model for much of this is Alain-Fournier's *Le Grand Meaulnes,* or *The Wanderer.*[5] Like *The Magus, Le Grand Meaulnes* is a first-person narrative most of which takes place around a school. Its main character sends the girl who loves and needs him to her ruin because he prefers the dreamlike to the real. Only when Yvonne resists him does he prize her. Having won her love, he holds her cheaply. In *The Aristos*, Fowles spoke of this longing for the unattainable girl and of its ruinous equation of sexual love with privation: "When Meaulnes eventually refound his *domaine perdu, domaine sans nom*, when at last he met the mysterious Yvonne de Galais again, what did he do? He ran away after the first night of their marriage." The tensional field generated by presence and absence is not merely academic. Alison's biddability and open, loving nature hurt her chances with Urfe by making her too easily available. Perhaps the true tension does not reside between presence and absence, but between Being and Nonbeing. Perhaps Urfe downgrades Alison's love, not because it comes easily, but because it comes at all. The familiar is not usually fine or beautiful to us; we crave the forbidden, the new, the unexplored.

Because sex works on the same glands and nerves as imaginative art, it exerts a strong spell upon a poet and student of literature, like Urfe. He has both the imagination and background to appreciate the masque built around him on Phraxos, and, at twenty-five, has also the excitement and freedom of an unknown future. Conchis tells him, "You have the one thing that matters. You have all your discoveries before you." But he doubts his ability to give these discoveries meaning. He calls Urfe disbelieving, self-defeating, and defensive, and he accuses him of lacking both imagination and patience. Clearly, the teacher has a great deal to learn. Elsewhere, he is called a masochist, and with good reason. His failure to follow through on his resolves, his frequent misjudgments, and his resenting Conchis, not for the pain Conchis inflicts on him, but that he stops inflicting it—these responses all invite misfortune. Fowles, of course, believes that the world is beautiful for those with beauty in their hearts, but that it is a wilderness and waste for the empty-hearted. Curiously, the disclaimers made by several characters about Urfe come close to Miranda's disclaimers about Clegg. Urfe is always scolded for wanting to satisfy his curiosity. In a world where hazard abounds and where mountebanks succeed, he should be looking for mysteries. What he needs is faith and imagination, not answers. He can only become human by waiving his requirement for factual truth and by accepting doubt. Once, he calls himself a *seeker*. But his unwillingness to suspend disbelief—uncommon in a poet—defeats his need to seek. Conchis's comparing him to a porcupine gives the lie to his self-defeating hunger for explanations: "You are like a porcupine. When that animal has its spines erect, it cannot eat. If you do not eat, you will starve. And your prickles will die with the rest of your body."

The art-life dualism that vitalizes Urfe's extended ordeal by art gains expression through his relationships with Alison Kelly and a young woman he meets first as Lily Montgomery, Conchis's dead fiancée of forty years before, and then comes to know as the actress Julie Holmes and the psychologist Vanessa Maxwell. Robert Scholes has summarized the fascination Lily holds for Urfe:

> Lily seems to be what he has always wanted. Her artificiality and unattainability, of course, make it safe for him to want her. She represents a narcistic gratification rather than a real engagement with another person. [6]

What robs his relation with her of reality is its lack of human content. Lily is sylphlike, gossamer, wispy. To spare Alison's feelings, he describes his friendship with her as "an asexual thing, a fascination of the mind." Ironically, the description fits the facts. When he tells her that she has him under her spell, she throws his words right back: "You have me just as much in your power." What she says is true. Conditioned and finally governed by the masque, their relationship cannot grow. It lacks the freedom of hazard. Urfe says elsewhere of her, "I realized everything with her was in parentheses. What she was outside those parentheses, I was no nearer to knowing." She has no being for him beyond the bounds set by the masque.

But while the masque hides her personality, Urfe's imagination rushes in to supply the missing colors and shades. Her white clothes invite him to simulate fantasies; pale and pitiless, she is a white witch whose cool, shifting glow lures and fascinates. One of her guises is that of Ashtaroth the

Unseen; like that of this goddess, her invisibility forms an important part of her mystery. The energy Urfe directs to her makes her the book's most intriguing figure. This intrigue, once again, mounts in direct ratio to her mystery. Like Daphne du Maurier's Rebecca, she is an enigmatic heroine whose virtue is always in question. Even when she betrays Urfe, she makes him wonder if her betrayals are forced on her. He can never gauge the freedom of her choices or her role in the masque. Though her acts seem to condemn her, he prefers to give her the benefit of any available doubt. Now Fowles once called Estella of *Great Expectations* Dickens's most realistic heroine, and he might have modeled Lily on her in part. For Urfe follows Pip by entertaining a destructive passion for a woman not worth his pains and sexually indifferent to him. Estella exists erotically to carry out Miss Havisham's revenge on men. Lily has the same instrumental existence. She tells Urfe several times she is dead, and the last thing she says in the role of Julie—in a voice "as hard as glass"—is, "There is no Julie."

If Nonbeing is Lily-Julie's chief attribute, Alison's is a concrete steadiness. The reader learns (Chapter Sixty-seven) that her name comes from the Greek *a* (without) *lyssa* (madness). Urfe says of her, "She was human warmth, normality, standard to go by," and he defines her "supreme virtue" as "a constant reality." "Her crystal core of nonbetrayal" certifies her as "a little piece of pure womankind," and she is cast as Reality in the masque, or Godgame, Conchis devises for Urfe. Choosing Alison, therefore, is a choice for life. The similarity between her name and that of the Wife of Bath, the Miller's Wife, and the heroine of the best-selling *Peyton Place* (1956) carves out a sexual context for this life.

She enters the novel inauspiciously, wearing a mackintosh, the uniform of the seedy and run-down in Joyce and Greene. She also wears a bruised, battered look expressive of a past that includes several jobs, affaires, and an abortion. Though confused, she is candid. She knows she has a good figure and pretty face, and she has the self-confidence to obey her impulses: "She liked doing things, and only then finding a reason for doing them." She stays with Urfe the same night they meet, and they start living together shortly thereafter. Their love grows spontaneously. They thrive together, complementing each other, making exciting self-discoveries, even reordering reality. In several passages that recall the honeymoon of Will and Anna Brangwen in *The Rainbow*, Fowles conveys the heavy animal sensation of two people sleeping, eating, and making love at all hours. Yet, as has been said, Urfe grabs his first chance to end this liaison and bolt to Greece.

After a break of nine months, Alison visits him in Greece for a weekend. The visit does not work out well for her. Hurt, she leaves abruptly and allegedly kills herself soon afterwards. Her initials are those of Anna Karenina, who also gave up all for love and then, regretting her mistake, committed suicide. Alison, too, talks of throwing herself under a train, as Anna did. But in our post-locomotive age, she works as an air hostess, and her love is only derailed temporarily. The report that Alison killed herself because of her broken affaire with Urfe turns out false. Meanwhile, during the months she is believed dead, she looms ever larger to Urfe. His escape is fatuous. His presence in Greece proves that he has to go abroad to get news from home and that, like Chestertonian man, he must travel toward home as to a foreign land. In the realm of human emotions, the shortest distance between two points is not a straight line.

A passage from Eliot's "Little Gidding" that Urfe reads soon after coming to Phraxos and that served as the epigraph to the movie version of *The Magus* charts the rough contours of Urfe's horizon:

> We shall not cease from exploration
> And the end of all our exploring
> Will be to arrive where we started
> And know the place for the first time.

These lines refocus the Alice-in-Wonderland motif that runs through the book. At first, the motif aligns with Urfe's escapism. Right after his arrival in Greece, Urfe feels "as gladly and unexpectantly disoriented, as happily and alertly alone, as Alice in Wonderland." Then, the passage from "Little Gidding" reminds us that the Queen of Hearts told Alice to run as fast as she can if she wants to stay in the same place. Alison's name also sounds like Alice's, and the central Australian town Alison and Urfe talk of visiting, Alice Springs, shows that even the parched Australian outback shimmers with wonder and flowing vitality. When Urfe sees a painting near the end of the book of "a little Alice-like girl," we know that Alison is close by. But before he can win her, he must, Humpty-Dumpty-like, crack the shell of his old life.

Urfe had asked Conchis in a waggish moment to be paid for acting in Conchis's metatheater. He is told, "You will receive the highest salary of all." Conchis wants nothing more (or less) for Urfe than a steady job, a home in the suburbs, and a family that loves him. Accustomed to scoffing at these middle-class values, Urfe learns that they do not come as easily or mindlessly as he had cynically imagined. Two family scenes are introduced in the book's closing chapters—an Oriental dish depicting a family of four having a meal together and, more prosaically, the side of a cereal package showing "a nauseatingly happy 'average' family" of four. Urfe's challenge is more adaptive than rebellious. The two family scenes help teach him that family life, though flawed and frustrating, is life's greatest gift. Whereas to accept it uncritically betokens a moral suicide, to reject it is madness. The psychological double game Urfe must play with himself recalls the following passage from *The Aristos:* "He [the Aristos] knows . . . that the true destiny of man is to become a magician." The rippling, singing balance Urfe aims for between life's many polarities affirms the solidity of the commonplace. It also makes the prosaic suburban routine of keeping a home together as challenging as that of the creative artist. In Urfe's case, the risks are higher, since he must summon the faith to work toward a goal not only out of view, but also perhaps out of reach. This faith must stem from his willingness to use himself as the raw material for his conjurer's trick of sharing his life. Fowles's looking-glass novel puts forth the bread-winner, not the artist or leader, as a heroic ideal.

II

Phraxos is a beautiful pine-covered island in the Aegean, about eight hours by ship from Athens. It is also unspoiled, idyllic, nearly untouched: "Its distinguishing characteristic . . . was silence . . . It was the world before the machine, almost before man." "Stupendously manless," it is an apt setting for a birth or transformation. But the birth takes Urfe by surprise. He finds his teaching a bore and, to give himself something to do, starts walking around the island. These walks immerse him in an ancestral and private past; he moves forward by moving backward. Unfortunately, the walks also betray signposts obviously planted by Fowles. Yet the authorial bullying is mitigated by the richness of the prose and by the powerful idea:

> I had the strangest feeling . . . of having entered a myth; a knowledge of what it was like . . . to have been young and ancient, a Ulysses on his way to meet Circe, a Theseus on his journey to Crete, an Oedipus still searching for his destiny. I could not describe it. It was not in the least a literary feeling, but an

intensely mysterious present and concrete feeling of excitement, of being in a situation where anything still might happen. As if the world had suddenly, during these last three days, changed from being the discovered to the still undiscovered.

One reason he finds his academic routine so dragging is that it makes him speak Basic English most of the time. This restraint, though, rivets his attention on certain basics of life he had earlier overlooked. He situates himself in nature for the first time and even sees himself as "the very first man" to stand on one of the island beaches. Nature stops being a passive background and throngs to life: "The hills were always intoxicatingly clean and light and remote. With no company but my own boredom, I began for the first time in my life to look at nature, and to regret that I knew its language as little as I knew Greek." This natural language he never masters. He needs more than nature's beauties for excitement. He fits nowhere and he has nowhere to go. Though exiled from the contemporary world, he finds the green innocence of Phraxos inadequate: "I was rootless. I rejected my own age, yet would not sink back into an older. So I ended like Sciron, a mid-air man." (This reference brings out Fowles's extraordinary care with incidentals: Sciron's plundering ways in Greek mythology prefigure Urfe's sexual and emotional preying upon young women; Sciron's becoming a tortoise after Theseus kills him points to both Urfe's shell of egotism and, as he later identifies with Theseus, his self-defeating nature.)

Urfe ends Part One with "a metaphysical sense of being marooned." He has no friends, he realizes that he writes bad poetry, and he is told that he may have syphilis. In his gloom, he considers suicide: "I hated myself. I had created nothing, I belonged to nothingness, to the *néant,* and it seemed to me that my own death was the only thing left that I could create." But no sooner does he decide to kill himself than he admits that he wants to die for effect, to create an impression: "It was a Mercutio death that I was looking for, not a real one." Then the mysteries start. What cancels his aesthetic suicide is the "intensely mysterious" voice of a girl. At first the mysteries stay within the estate of Maurice Conchis, a rich recluse who owns part of the island and who may have collaborated with the Nazis. Before the novel ends, these mysteries, or games, or masques, or psychodramas, or experiments in metatheater, break out of the island and take half the world as their setting. The games are all part of a supervening Godgame, an elaborate, formalized test for Urfe. Scholes's etymological reading of the name, Phraxos, shows that the godgame has an end in view: "Phraxos is derived from the Greek word $\Phi PAZ\Omega$, which in one of its forms means to devise or plan for a person, to design or intend something for him."[8] Yet, both improvised and scripted, the godgame allows for the unforeseen while retaining its sharp focus.

The Godgame leaves you breathless and confused, weary and fascinated. Roles in it are hard to assign. Conchis seems to steer the charade, but insists he is merely an actor. Urfe calls himself a victim, and he can back his claim by showing how the masque batters and terrifies him and then saps him of dignity, meaning, and hope. As with Miranda in *The Collector,* his celebration of the end of one ordeal marks the onset of another. But here the comparison with Miranda ends. Unlike her, he is free to walk out of his ordeal at any time. What he has not learned is that the charade is no mere display piece. A pioneer in drama, Conchis claims to have carried experimental theater beyond Artaud, Pirandello, and Brecht. His metatheater, by doing away with the audience, makes everybody an actor: all the world's a stage. And since actors traffic in poetic rather than factual truth, they may lie. Conchis tells Urfe rightly that his role at Bourani, Conchi's estate, has no name.

The Godgame brings together a storm of wild, fantastic

scenes incorporating symbol, myth, and allegory. Music, cinema, the stage, narration, and sculpture all share in turning the known into the undiscovered. Time and space play tricks. Everything Urfe has lived by and taken for granted goes awry. He is told, "In your role you do not know what you can believe and what you cannot." He agrees; he calls his metaphysical hazing "the strangest maze in Europe" and "a sort of game inside a game." But this nest of games departs from reality without rejecting it. The masque's intersecting arcs of belief and disbelief, illusion and reality, and trust and deceit blur the line between mystery and meaning. Fowles dives below the surface of life to portray it poetically. His subject matter—unenvironmented, acausal reality—calls for many narrative modes to keep pace with the expanding psychodrama. At times the materials seem to get out of hand; the Godgame can be subtle and obvious, graceful and clumsy, all at once. Fowles needs this indeterminacy because what interests him is often too intangible and shadowy for direct statement. In spite of his spectacular effects, his art is that of the barely comprehended. He does not argue nor demonstrate. Less eager to impart a message than to distill a highly complex experience, he speaks through the medium of the Godgame. The life depicted in *The Magus* is not the life British novels usually depict. But the Godgame creates new narrative possibilities and opens new approaches to problems in communication. It speaks to the mind while addressing the soul. The characters have two lives—one observable and the other secret and hidden, even from themselves. Its rhythmically orchestrated network of associations gives the Godgame access into this vaulting, downthrusting, interlocking reality.

As if the Godgame were not baffling enough in its own right, the masquers prime Urfe psychologically for it. Conchis tells him that it is being staged to cure Lily's schizophrenia. He addresses him as a colleague and fellow diagnostician, making him privy to the supposed particulars of Lily's case. He will flatter him by calling him psychic; he will pander to his intellectual vanity. Then Lily-Julie and her twin sister Rose-June will duck in and out of *their* roles. In one moment, they accuse Urfe of leaguing with Conchis against them. Then, they puff up his ego by asking his protection and telling him that they count on him. But no sooner does he feel clever, strong, and safe than he is upended. The wildest surprises in the Godgame come when he feels most secure.

These surprises, besides stepping up the action, make for thematic depth. Fowles repeats Joyce's practice in *Ulysses* of comparing his modern-day protagonist to a mythical hero. Urfe compares himself to Oedipus, Orestes, Orpheus, Theseus, Adonis, Candide, Adam, Robinson Crusoe, and the self-destroying rebel-son, Icarus. Several Shakespearean echoes are sounded. The parallel to Caliban recurs from *The Collector*. Urfe is also likened to Iago and Malvolio, Shakespeare's two leading figures of vice, egotism, and immorality. These figures are also outsiders, and, like them, Urfe chafes at being left out. His exclusions happen explosively. Several masquers, including Conchis, break into the room where he is about to take Lily-Julie to bed. Ensnared, deprived, and shamed, Urfe both looks and feels like Mars trapped in *his* lust by Hephaestus's invisible net. That Mars is the god of war looks back to Conchis's calling war a male failing grounded in a disrespect for personal relationships. It also knits with the military background of Urfe's family and with the book's numerous battle scenes to portray life without love as a battlefield.

The comparisons with Oedipus and Theseus, antiquity's most famous searchers, are just as rewarding, even though Urfe seems more searched out than searching. He is most real in mid-search; like Oedipus, answers and formal endings lay him low. He must see that the Godgame has no end and that the maze has no center. His taking a loose thread from Lily-Julie's dress as from Ariadne's spool is cheap literary escapism. It reveals him in his usual pose of easing a personal stress by pretending to be a character in a book. Today's Theseus must wander "the interminable maze of echoes" haunting the Godgame. The numerous references to rats, the labyrinth's sudden turns and twists, and Urfe's sinking self-esteem contrast him with Crete's brave young soldier-king. Ratlike, he finds himself led along byways marked out by others. The novel's technical borrowings from crime fiction bring the following comment on rats from Eric Ambler's *Epitaph for a Spy* (1938) within Urfe's sphere:

> It is well known. The French criminal is a snake, the American criminal is a wolf, and the English criminal is a rat. Snakes, wolves, and rats. The rat is a very simple animal. He fights only when he is in a corner. At other times he merely nibbles.[9]

Easily duped, selfish without being brave, and a feeder on the garbage of his escapist fantasies, Urfe, like a disease-carrying rat, infects others. He cheats his students by teaching his classes badly; he causes Alison grief; he is told by Lily-Julie that he drives her mad. He cannot stop causing pain; even after learning, near the end, an "eleventh commandment" that forbids committing pain, he hurts two women who care deeply for him.

Another classical parallel that discredits Urfe is the one with Orpheus. Orpheus is the great singer and poet of ancient times; Urfe, whose name sounds like that of Orpheus, is no poet at all. Bad faith costs both men their women: Orpheus leads his beloved Eurydice out of Tartarus but loses her when he turns to make sure she is still following him. Urfe is faithlessness incarnate. He calls himself an atheist and a traitor on the same page, and Lily attacks him for being too literal and fact-hunting: "Why must you always know where you are? Why have you no imagination, no humor, no patience . . . ? You have no imagination . . . no poetry . . . That is why you are so treacherous." Ironically, this unpoetic creature climbs Parnassus, shrine of Apollo and the legendary muses of Greek poetry. The climbing episode is crucial, taking place exactly midway through the book. Alison has come to visit Urfe. Her visit is redolent of beginnings, resurrection, and precivilized experience in general. Parnassus conveys a human, not a literary lesson. In their joint climb, Urfe and Alison go from wintry bleakness ("the wind cut like January in England") to brightness and warmth ("Soon we are walking in sunshine again.... Everywhere there were flowers"). The road to the top, though gusty, rocky, and hidden by fog, brings rich rewards if traversed with somebody special. Sharing the physical dangers of climbing brings Alison and Urfe closer. Reaching the top literally puts the world at their feet. Urfe mentions "a delicious intellectual joy marrying and completing the physical one."

After their climb, the couple swim naked in a wooded area likened to Eden. Alison has responded livingly to the intense sharing expressive of the weekend. She clears the hurdles set up by Urfe's psychological thralldom to the Godgame. Obeying her warm, healthy instincts, she does not ask him to explain why he shrunk from sex with her. Explanations, she knows, are secondary to human touch. ("Not now," she says. "Please not now. Whatever's happened, come and make love to me.") Yet Urfe's calling the Eden-like outing "an intensely literary moment" shows his unreadiness to follow her lead. His human failure matches his artistic one; he fails as a poet for the same reason that he fails as a man. He repeats his literary shortcomings by failing the test of Parnassus, the wellspring of an art form devoted to tightening man's hold on life. Stung and bewildered, Alison leaves Greece soon after he explains his interest in Conchis's psychodramas and especially in Lily. The gravity of his failure shows vividly in the events following Parnassus. Urfe's returning Alison's love might have ended the Godgame on the spot. Instead, the Godgame steps up its pace and grows more physical.

First, Urfe hears that Alison had become so saddened by his treatment of her that she killed herself. Reliving the German occupation of Greece in 1943, he sees a squad of Nazi soldiers savage a Greek peasant. He gets hurt falling over a trip wire. His failure to sustain the heights scaled at Parnassus foreshadows his fall, here and elsewhere. The equilibrium must be restored: Parnassus presumes a Tartarus. Urfe is indeterminate man. Endowed with both transcendental and descendental qualities, he spends time underground and explores his cavernous heart. This self-exploration, though painful, is essential. The novel's topography traces Urfe's costive growth. The last chapter takes place in Regent's Park. The terrain has flattened; the mood has become more familiar and relaxed; the setting is neither exotic nor poetically charged. Yet its openness, its shareability, and Urfe's proposal of marriage to the resurrected Alison all signal a new ability to be on a level with common experience. Though the Godgame is without end, it no longer need rattle Urfe between the poles of high and low, intense joy and despair.

III

The mystery man at the center of the mysterious, expanding Godgame and the book's most enigmatic figure is Maurice Conchis. Fowles builds him up before he comes into the book through the local gossip Urfe hears about him from the villagers. Conchis, who likes his name pronounced *conscious,* suggests a limit in human achievement. More revealing than this on-the-nose pun is the parallel with classical Greek *conchis,* meaning seashell, or conch. The parallel touches on the way shells pick up sound, that is, their visual emptiness and acoustical richness. (Fowles used to pick up such shells along the beaches round Spetsai, his model for the "fenced island" of Phraxos.) An extremely rich and accomplished man of about sixty, Conchis has won his spurs as a musician, scholar, businessman, physician, and art collector. He owns original works by Modigliani, Rodin, and Bonnard; he fought in the trenches in the 1914-18 War; he hates novels. If Conrad's Mr. Kurtz represents the fag end of nineteenth-century European imperialism, Conchis stands for a later and more broadly cultural tradition, that of 1890-1930. He speaks French, English, and demotic Greek fluently, and in his veins run Greek, Italian, English, and even Celtic blood. Urfe's first glimpse of him emits a primitive intensity akin to terror:

> He was nearly completely bald, brown as old leather, short and spare, a man whose age was impossible to tell; perhaps sixty, perhaps seventy . . . . The most striking thing about him was the intensity of his eyes; very dark brown, staring, with a simian penetration . . . eyes that seemed not quite human.

> He had a bizarre family resemblance to Picasso; saurian as well as simian . . . who had discarded everything that lay between him and his vitality. A monkey-glander, essence of queen bees; and intense by choice and exercise as much as by nature.

Urfe speaks of him as "polyhedral" and finds himself struck by his learning and his mysticism. Mysticism comes easily to Conchis because of his love for mystery. (Conchis is Fowles's spokesman for the life-giving power of mystery in the novel.) A lover of mystery, he exudes mystery himself. Is he the Godgame's director? scriptwriter? or merely an actor? He refers to himself as both Zeus and Prospero. He also claims to have been shot by a German firing squad in 1943, but his gravestone, marked 1949, suggests a different truth.

These puzzles make Conchis the best candidate for the book's title character. The epigraph, from Arthur Edward Waite's *The Key to the Tarot,* defines the *Magus* as a "Magician, or Juggler, the caster of the dice and mountebank in the world of vulgar trickery." In a world of frauds, the Magus is the archfraud, the trickster or joker supreme. Urfe calls Conchis "a genius among practical jokers" and often speaks of being tricked by him. His japes help Conchis play an important social role. People like Clegg and Urfe prove the necessity for Magi. A cultural Gresham's Law holds true today. Low standards and inferior cultures drive out superior ones. An educated man like Urfe acts no better than Clegg because today's consumer mentality exerts more force on personal choice than beauty, goodness, and justice. Magi retard this trend.

Fowles never analyzes Conchis's mystery or power. He does connect much of it, though, with music. If Clegg's weakness depended largely on his being a "visual," as Miranda calls him, then Conchis stands at an opposite pole. As the conch parallel suggests, his strength comes from his immersion in sound. His first memory is of hearing his mother singing; he becomes an expert in bird songs; he studies music for many years. He plays the harpsichord "as if there were no barrier between him and the music." He sacrifices none of life's richness to surface glamor or slickness of technique. Thus life makes a deeper impression on him, and he has more to offer life. His relationship with his former fiancée takes place in a musical climate:

> Our two families grew very close. I accompanied Lily, we sometimes played duets, sometimes her father would join us, sometimes the two mothers would sing. We discovered a whole new continent of sound.

Music is not Conchis's exclusive domain. The sound of Lily-Julie playing a recorder leads Urfe to the room where he first sees her, and it is while listening to music that he decides to make sense of the wreckage of his life. Plato claims that music has a harmony and order that, when learned, could help form a moral life; the harmoniously put-together person will avoid immorality and injustice. Fowles both endorses and extends this view of music. Music can promote sanity and health at *all* levels. It civilizes the masculine virtues of bravery, endurance, and ambition. The very act of listening to music requires a patience and talent alien to the combativeness of the market-place. This blend of activity and passiveness, of interpreting the sound and letting it have its way, carrying us along, refines the feeling. "You make words seem shabby things," Urfe tells Conchis after hearing him play Bach on the harpsichord. Music puts no barrier of meaning between player and hearer. Its semantics and its syntax both inhere in its sounds. Blending form and content, substance and symbol, it overrides linguistic differences. This universality builds a mood, freshens the spirit, and describes a reality all at once.

Swathed and nourished by music, Conchis is more clever, adaptable, and innovative than anyone else Urfe meets. Yet his powers are not just mental; he is no disembodied mind. As Urfe's notation of his polyhedral nature implies, he has run the gamut of human experience. He has a fierce, apelike look, the reverse of spirituality, and, as his scars and war stories show, he has undergone horrid physical suffering. His alleged autobiography—the one he unravels to Urfe, anyway—has four major movements. Each achieves a new reference for life by retreating from reason and social convention into mystery. The first movement includes his courtship and engagement with Lily Montgomery, Lily's death by typhus in 1915, and Conchis's brief turn as a combat soldier. The movement culminates in the battle of Neuve Chapelle, where Conchis feigns death and then gains "an intense new conviction" of life's preciousness. As happens so often in Fowles, the conviction comes in a moment of terror. The butchery of war makes England's becoming a Prussian colony preferable to "the blood, the gaping holes, the bones sticking out of flesh, the stench of burnt intestines" that go with war. After Neuve Chapelle, Conchis deserts from the British army, lives in South America, returns to Europe to take an M.D. degree, and learns the harpsichord. While in Paris, along with several other doctors, he founds the Society of Reason. Its bullying tone, promise of a golden age, and stress on the partnership of science and government give the Society's policy statement the shrillness of a Mosley manifesto. Conchis's health, meanwhile, has been failing. He is told to relax more and work less. After a quiet year or so, he meets two extraordinary men—the Count Alphonse de Deukans, with whom he has "the most remarkable friendship" of his life, and a mad Norweigan mystic who meets God in Conchis's presence.

The outlandishly wealthy Count stands for extreme comfort, leisure, and self-indulgence. He is not merely a collector, but a collector of collections. His museumlike castle in eastern France, Givray-le-Duc, houses painting, sculpture, and musical instruments from all over the world. The most prized object in his hoard, though, is a lifesize doll fitted with a dagger to stab the groin of anybody who tries to embrace her. This decadence, de Deukans's misogyny, and the extreme luxury of the *château* spell out a rotten-ripeness. De Deukans's life-style requires abundant domestic service. It has no place in post-1914, that is, democratic, Europe. "Unasked," a 1964 poem by Fowles, berates the criminal inequity of keeping up palaces like Givray-le-Duc in a world gripped by poverty, overpopulation, and maleducation: "I do not ask our charming host . . . how he dare presume / there is a hovel in the world / where those who starve are not his victims." [10] De Deukans's death in 1922, the same day his collection burns, is long over-due. Conchis speaks of his "archducal dignity," and he dies in a chauffeured car. Far from being unrelated, these data join him to the Archduke Franz Ferdinand, whose murder in a chauffeured limousine in 1914 started World War I and changed Europe.

The second major influence on Conchis from this period is Henrik Nygaard, a Norwegian ship's engineer gone blind and turned hermit and religious mystic. Conchis meets him by chance when his research in birds' songs sends him to northern Norway. Nygaard believes in divine cruelty. The belief that God wants him to suffer stops him from having his eyes examined. As scornful of hazard as de Deukans, he spurns all offers of help. Where he differs from de Deukans is in his faith. His madness has discovered a mystery to live by—that of an obscure divine wrath. Conchis sees him meeting God, and the meeting is mystical, vital, and powerful beyond the scope of reason. Science, Conchis sees, cannot compass reality. Nygaard's meeting with God, ignoring all criteria of verifiability, both irradiates and refreshes life. Sometimes the simplest truths are the best: faith can work miracles. Thanks to Nygaard, Conchis keeps trying to edge Urfe toward belief and also toward a mode of perception where the inner eye takes over. Faith gives the strength to move forward; even a pretended belief is better than none. Conchis tests Urfe's faith by asking him to believe that Nygaard's meeting with God, de Deukans's death, and the burning of Givray-le-Duc all hap-pened on the same day—17 August 1922. Conchis claims to be the only link between these events, and, indeed, the date seems to have no historical importance. Then why did Fowles choose it? Only a rough, incomplete answer suggests itself. 1922 is the publication year of revolutionary works in drama, fiction, and poetry—Pirandello's *Henry IV*, Joyce's *Ulysses,* and Eliot's *The Waste Land*—that, rather than denying the past, show how the past lives. This fusion of tradition and experiment could well mark the start of a new European epoch for Fowles. It certainly provides an artistic model for *The Magus.*

But if 1922 marked a new start, the 1939-45 War brought wholesale death. The stages of the masque mirror stages in (European) man's changing awareness of the world. The next key episode in Conchis's life came during the German occupation of Phraxos in 1943. Reacting to local pressures, Conchis had agreed to become mayor of the village. Soon after he took office, four German soldiers were shot by Cretan guerrillas. The guerrillas were caught and arrested. Then the sadistic colonel of the German garrison tried to get Conchis to club two of them to death with a rifle butt. When Conchis refused, he was shot by a firing squad along with eighty hostages. Clubbing the two prisoners to death would have saved these eighty lives. But joining the ranks of his countrymen vindicated freedom of choice. Conchis did *not* take life in order to save life. He claims that his decision sprang immediately and irresistibly out of the core of things. "My reason has repeatedly told me I was wrong. Yet my total being still tells me I was right." Urfe's feeling for the issues at stake in 1943 sharpens when he is seized and cuffed about by some actors impersonating Nazi troops.

This steepening typifies the Godgame. Either before or after each of Conchis's reminiscences, an item from the reminisence haunts Urfe. These hauntings or echoes are unpredictable. A sensory datum can materialize; sometimes a character or even a whole episode will leap to life. Conchis's summary of the 1914-18 War describes nationalism as a reeking pile of dung and charred, rotting flesh. The same night Urfe hears the story of Neuve Chapelle, he smells an atrocious stench outside his window while "Tipperary" pipes in the distance. Then Lily Montgomery, Conchis's dead financée, played by "Julie Holmes," comes into the action. Later, Conchis explains how de Deukans charmed him in his Oriental garden thirty years before while he, Conchis, charms and *disorients* Urfe. The echoes boom still deeper. Conchis plays the harpsichord, owns a *château,* and has far-reaching business holdings. Also, he met de Deukans at twenty-five, Urfe's age when he comes to Bourani. These echoes or hauntings emphasize the moral lessons embedded in Conchis's narratives. The past invades the present; psychic experience becomes material; story changes into fact. Urfe, meanwhile, becomes better conditioned for reality. Set wondering where body ends and mind begins, he tears loose from his cynicism. He learns to live with doubt and hazard.

These autobiographical reminiscences are very taut, dramatic, and colorful. But they gain added sting from their telling. Conchis's language—formal, strong, slightly stilted, richly allusive—has a powerful eloquence. Urfe notes that the autobiographies, even certain phrases, sound prepared. Conchis does remember the past with minute detail; names, dates, places, and features of natural landscape come effortlessly to mind. His near-total recall of events forty years in the past is staggering. We share Urfe's skepticism. No figure of realism, Conchis is more magus than storyteller. The God-game, a paradigm of reality, is subtle and obvious, graceful and clumsy. Conchis teaches by mystifying, entertaining, and shocking. These techniques, while maddening to Urfe, show him how to reason and fact increase unreality and also fuel the imagination.

But the hauntings and a gripping speaking style are not Conchis's only dramatic resources. He times his surprises well, and he knows how to pace a narrative. He will interrupt a story to fetch brandy or an *objet,* and during his absence Urfe will think about what he has heard and try to fit it into his own storehouse of perceptions. These absences also increase suspense, because Conchis's theatrical flair makes it impossible for Urfe to predict the outcome of any reminiscence. But above all, Conchis's absences break his reminiscences into movements or parts, a technique that both organizes Urfe's responses and sharpens moral statement. Sometimes, Conchis will reinforce a point with an illustrative example. Slides and films accompany his story of the Phraxian occupation; to clarify the injustice of war, he tricks Urfe into rolling a pair of loaded dice with death as the stakes. Sometimes, Lily listens along with Urfe to a narrative and by facial expression will steer him into a desired reaction. Considering the energy that goes into these interpolated autobiographies of Conchis, Urfe's scant moral progress speaks poorly for his moral fiber.

IV

But Urfe's seeing his ordeal through takes character. Like Job, he weathers a storm of setbacks and emerges with more faith than before. The hardship that does not destroy, strengthens. Though mean and boring most of the way, he does become self-acting. *The Magus* moves to a climax of recognition and resolve. Urfe chooses Alison over the false flowers, Lily and Rose, and he has gained the self-esteem to make Alison choose *him*. When told that he has to gain back Alison's love, he says, "There's gaining back to be done on both sides." *The Magus* is full of human warmth and attack. Yet how much of it is wasted effort? Does Urfe justify the time, care, and talent lavished on him by Conchis? by Fowles? The cost in money, talent, and effort that went into researching Urfe's personality and then devising an appropriate God-game for him adds to a fortune. To write off this expense as a loss, though, in Fowles's view is to hamper social progress. All reform starts with the self—what one is and what one wants.

Self-discovery underlies all public reform and planning. The Godgame is both a preparation for and a distillation of life. Like life, it is both fixed and free. Prank and lesson, knockabout and melodrama, it combines elements of improvisation and formal ritual. Urfe, it is worth repeating, can walk out of it any time. Yet he resents Conchis more for dismantling it than for using it to make him suffer.

When Urfe, puzzling his centricity in the Godgame, asks Conchis, "Why me?" he is answered, "Why anyone? Why anything?" As an annual rite, the English master at the Lord Byron School automatically becomes the subject of Conchis's masque. Conchis and his confederates, then, surrender themselves cheerfully to hazard. Saint Augustine once said that God loves each of us as an only child. Only a Godlike sensibility could give so much attention to an ordinary hunk of clay like Urfe. Anyone can love a hero; to love Urfe takes a God. The divine makes no exclusions, loving man while knowing the worst. The novel is steeped in commonness. Like Roman Polanski's film, *Knife in the Water,* it starts with a prosaic encounter, drifts into terror, and then comes back to the ordinary. Fog-wrapped London, with its fishy gray tones, replaces the hard, bright colors of sunny Greece. Alison comes back to Urfe, "quietly . . . . simply," in a drab cafeteria, and then he sits with her on a park bench:

> All the time I had expected some spectacular reentry, some mysterious call . . . . Not this. And yet, as I stared at her, unable to speak, at her bright look, the smallest smile, I understood that this was the only possible way of return; her rising into this most banal of scenes, this most banal of London, this reality as plain and dull as wheat.

It has been said that natural law is indwelling, not imposed. At the end, the pageant and machinery of the Godgame leave the scene, and life takes its own measure. Urfe is on his own.

His seeing that the restoration of simplicity could only happen simply denotes real growth. According to Scholes, it makes a magus out of him:

> The world is not dead and nauseating. It is alive and unknowable and thoroughly invigorating. To accept its unfathomable mystery one must become equally unfathomable, one must accept one's own mystery and become a magician.[11]

Truths that come easily to some only reach others after great toil. The crucial difference, as has been pointed out, is faith. Faith strengthens. A world where nothing has fixed value and where illusion blurs with reality teaches the need to suspend reason. If truth and fact part company, as the Godgame proves, then we must always keep a foot in the aesthetic sphere. Some trace of pretense, even of self-pretense, touches all out acts; we always act a little. In the book's last scene, Urfe is able to mock and make love at the same time. Living for the moment, he commits himself to Alison while forgetting the hazard-filled future. Knowing reason to be regulative rather than constitutive, he has the faith to move forward in doubt. Acting out of need has made him a magus. He rivals Conchis as the book's title character. The magic he practices on himself is a beneficial white magic that helps him live. The time setting of the final scene, Hallowe'en, both adds to the unreality that pervades the scene and counterweights the deadly serious reality of the moment.

Fowles always encourages means-oriented living. The priority given means over ends in *The Magus* takes different forms from the one seen in the book's last chapter. Urfe speaks wrongly of "one last trick," "the grand finale," and "Conchis's last joke." The Godgame has no end; the maze has no center. Conchis had said, "No good play has a real curtain . . . . It is acted, and then it continues to act." The last scene in *The Magus* crowns the action, but it also leaves plenty of life untouched. To deny that every end is also a beginning denies both life's inexhaustibility and the chance ordering of human events; the Shakespearean metaphor, "All the world's a stage," holds true to the end. Nevertheless, the closing pages of *The Magus* have stirred more debate than anything else in the book. Do Alison and Urfe get together? or do they part? Without dissolving human complexities, Chapter Seventy-eight respects the reader's longing for decisive action and sharp-cut issues. The postscript, *cras amet qui numquam amavit quique amavit cras amet,* stresses renewal and rebirth through love: tomorrow he may love who has never loved, and he who *has* loved may love tomorrow, too. His ordeal by art has not broken Urfe. The individual cannot be measured or put down by intellectual systems. Though The Godgame rakes Urfe's flesh, it uncovers a living heart. It also pays him the tribute of giving him a chance to win Alison.

Like Joyce's *A Portrait,* the novel ends just before a decisive act is undertaken. Like *Ulysses,* it uses complexity to make the simple point that people need other people. *The Magus* is dedicated to Astarte, Phoenician goddess of love and fertility and also the mother of mystery. Though Diana, the chaste huntress, appears in the action, Fowles's desire to blend fertility with mystery stops him from dedicating the book to her. Besides, Diana's chastity goes against the idea of self-realization through sex, insisted on throughout and made prominent in the last chapter. The setting for this chapter, a park or public garden, could not be more fitting for a rebirth or revelation. And Fowles has orchestrated his motifs so as to lead rhythmically to this Joycean moment. Urfe's crying for the first time when he learns of Alison's death in Chapter Fifty-one constitutes a melting into life. He comes back to London in Chapter Sixty-nine in despair; he has no job, he feels betrayed by the newly resurrected Alison, his year in Greece has made him a stranger in his own land. Yet within three pages of calling himself "an old, old man," he mentions "a feeling that haunted me as the embryo grows in the mother's womb." An Alice-in-Wonderland reversal of the myth of the eternal return sends him home to be born. This slow, dragging, inconsequential-looking rebirth begins with the family. First, there are the family scenes depicted on the Oriental dish and on the cereal package. Next, Urfe meets two frumps—his landlady, Joan Kemp, and the young Scots ragamuffin, Jojo. These females help launch him into life because he helps and befriends them without asking anything in return. His not using either Kemp or Jojo brings rewards. Because he demands nothing from them, good things come his way. Kemp gives him the mothering his nerves need, and Jojo companions him as a sister.

Chapter Seventy-eight joins this birth motif to several others. It is set in Regent's Park, facing the white marble buildings comprising Cumberland Terrace. Urfe knows that Conchis may be watching, even photographing, his encounter with Alison. He fights theater with theater. Taking reality on its own terms, he plays a final impromptu scene with Alison. The scene finds them acting and not acting, playing roles but speaking from the heart. They know that love is a hornet's nest but also that to reject it is wasteful madness. Urfe has a clear view of himself and his prospects. He owns up to his faults; he admits his ongoing obsession with Lily-Julie. Then he throws out the possibility that he has started to see the importance of personal relations. On this skimpy evidence, Alison is to declare for or against him forever. For the benefit of the possible onlookers in Cumberland Terrace, he tells her that when he turns from her, she is to follow him and take his arm. Then he will slap her face very hard ("It won't hurt me half as much as it hurts you"). They will leave Regent's Park by different routes and meet later—without stopping to communicate with anybody—in the waiting room of Paddington

Station. The parting scene in the park will trick Conchis into giving up hope for the relationship. The joker will be beaten at his own game; common, everyday experience will outshine the spectacular. Conchis's metatheater will fade into the drab prose of Paddington, and the lovers can forget the Godgame.

Scholes has noted the looking-glass parallel with classical literature the book's last scene completes:

> In the Greek romances and their imitations, hero and heroine fall in love to begin the story but are prevented from consummating their union until the end. In **The Magus** we begin with a sexual union and it is love which must wait for consummation until the end of the book.[12]

Scholes does well to say that the lovers get together at the end. Though the book ends in Regent's Park with their walking away from each other, they have been primed for renewal through love. Joy and pain, birth and death (the season is mid-fall) interlock. The novel's Alice-in-Wonderland structure-frame reduces Lily-Julie and Rose-June to Tweedledee and Tweedledum. What is more important, it turns Urfe's walking away from Alison into a walking toward. Urfe's slapping Alison's face instigates new life, and his walking away, Orpheus-like, "not once looking back," signals new faith. Whether he is acting for his own benefit or someone else's, his action is both vigorous and open-ended. He commits himself without asking for proofs or guarantees.

The meeting place Urfe suggests for himself and Alison, the waiting room of Paddington Station, unifies the novel. *Waiting* is the most important word in the book. Urfe must learn how to wait. Midway through the book, when asked what he is doing, he answers, "Nothing . . . . Waiting," as if the two activities were the same. A poem he writes describes him as "the fool that . . . . never learns to watch and wait." Toward the end, when he threatens to stop waiting for Alison to reveal herself, he is told, "Then she will be well rid of you," and, "Wait as long as Alison makes you wait." At the end of a meal at Bourani in Chapter Seventeen, he had said, "I was content to wait," and Lily materializes in the next sentence. Waiting staves off the evil bred by activity. Activity in the novel, especially when resulting from cynicism or impatience, usually undoes Urfe. Whenever he acts rashly, he either looks silly or defeats his interests. He must learn the uses of passiveness. Much of his ordeal at Phraxos demands quiet listening, and he spends most of his time in London waiting for Alison. Henrik Nygaard had called out, before his mystical meeting with God in Chapter Forty-four, "I am waiting . . . . I am purified . . . . I am prepared." For him, waiting precedes and perhaps underlies purification and readiness. It takes a great deal of waiting to purge Urfe of his actionism, acquisitiveness, and treachery. A former English master at Lord Byron School warns him in Chapter Five, "Beware of the waiting room." Three chapters later, waiting saves his life. About to kill himself by squeezing a dead branch against the trigger of a shotgun, he waits: "I waited . . . . I waited, I waited . . . . I waited." Waiting precludes the black moment of death and restores him to hazard. He learns to equate it with faith. One of the first things he tells Alison in the last chapter is, "I'm waiting. As I've been waiting these last three and a half months." Rather than imposing his personality and his needs, he has let life happen to him. The ache of anticipation, meanwhile, has turned his waiting into a waiting *for*. Everyone gains a bargain. Urfe acquires faith; Alison, the awaited person, takes on greater reality because of the psychic energy poured into his waiting for her. Fowles's personal life also points to a happy future for Alison and Urfe. The novel's final waiting place, Paddington, is London's station for the west of England—where Fowles spent his happiest days as an adolescent, where he lives now, and where his ancestors came from.

Paddington Station's waiting room thus stands as a benediction, a forecast, and a happy start. Urfe's waiting has been redeemed.

Passivity lies at the core of *The Magus*. Related to waiting is Conchis's remark, "There are times when silence is a poem." Urfe stops writing poetry and then learns how to wait. *The Magus* is a bristling, action-crammed novel about silence; silence ultimately describes a noisy, bustling age. Fowles's calling *The Magus* "a fable about the relationship between man and his conception of God"[13] turns on this very point. Not acting creates a vacuum into which the life-giving realities of hazard and mystery may rush and fecundate.

A silence that proves creative is the one binding the players in Conchis's metatheater. This cast includes the staff of the Lord Byron School, several former teachers there, various Phraxians, including the local postal authorities, a smattering of Londoners Urfe meets when he goes back home, and several crews of actors from all over Western Europe. That Conchis and his masquers conduct the same rite every year with the new English master of Lord Byron School proves the Godgame a going, thriving concern. Yet no rite is comparable to any other. The reason for this lies in the religious sphere. The Godgame mirrors the Christian cycle of penitence, purgatory, and redemption·through rebirth. Each lesson or course of instruction, purging, and purifying differs from the next because each person is unique. Since each English teacher, novice, or acolyte comes to Conchis with different needs and backgrounds, no two translations can be the same.

No former novice or subject can help his successor. The Godgame discourages the comparing of notes: with truth situational and relative, no explanation holds for more than one person; life's greatest lessons can only be lived, not taught nor shown. Silence confirms the worth of the Godgame. But it does not exhaust the conspiracy of silence linking the masquers. Human nature is not very nice. One of our more disagreeable traits is to weather an ordeal and then wish it on a successor rather than softening it or doing away with it. The society that breaks the individual is made up of broken individuals. Urfe stands in the same relation to his predecessors as his successor stands to him:

> I disliked Mitford [the subject of the Godgame of 1952] because he was crass and mean, but even more because he was a caricature, an extension, of certain qualities in myself.

> Faced with the guileless, earnest Briggs I felt a little of what Mitford must have felt with me: a malicious amusement.

The process by which a victim becomes a disciple and then an oppressor gains voice in a parable Urfe reads (Chapter Sixty-five) called "The Prince and the Magician." A young prince is told by his father the king that princesses, islands, and God do not exist. He soon meets a man with his coatsleeves rolled back who convinces him that his father lied. Moreover, the stranger claims to be God. When the prince goes back home and explains the incident, he hears that the man who claimed to be God was a magician and that *all* kings and gods are merely magicians. "There is no truth beyond magic," says the king. No reality underlies appearance; the phenomenon is all. Truth and fact do not exist objectively but inhere, instead, in the perceiver. At the end of the parable, the disillusioned prince has already started to become a magician. He risks that his father was lying and that the man who claimed to be God had nothing up his rolled-back sleeves. (*The Aristos* speaks of the Bet Situation, "a problem that we cannot and never shall solve, but about which we ought to come to some conclusion," as basic to life.) Better to be a king or a god than a brooding cynic, even if you do not have all the credentials for the post. Rather than wallowing in doubt, the young prince starts wearing a regal aspect. Soon he will live his regal fiction.

The Prince becomes a ruler, to begin with, when he accepts the discrepancy between *is* and *ought*. To set up an intercognition and an interaction with the unknowable and then to live freely in this tensional field—these psychic acrobatics make the prince a realist, fantasist, king, god, and magus in one miraculous stroke. His duty to his subjects? The burden of self-being is a private challenge. Nobody can pursue the phantom of another personality. His subjects must adapt to uncertainty and hazard just as he and his father before him did.

The Magus pulses with human warmth and wisdom. Here is vision, artistry, and compassion. Bergonzi's complaint, "At the end the elaborate, pretentious glittering structure collapses into anticlimax,"[14] has little force. The novel could not have ended any other way. Nor is it marred by manic inclusiveness. Fowles has something to say, and he knows how to say it. Though innovative, he respects the ancient art of storytelling. He uses a plot, a temporal and spatial structure, a central action, and well-hewn, vividly imagined characters. Rather than satisfying the Now Culture's desire for instant gratification, he roots himself in the past and looks toward the future. *The Magus* resonates. His vocabulary, syntax, and learning serve this resonance. No technical obsessiveness weakens his grasp of life's basic enduring simplicities. Style and imagination work together; the plot and the incidents that move it along claim equal attention. The book's assuredness, together with its range and sustained strength, touches rare depths of belief. These virtues make *The Magus* a civilizing force as well as a work of high literary art.

NOTES TO CHAPTER 3

1. Guy Davenport, "Lulu in Bombazeen," *The Nation*, 2 December 1969, p. 1,223; Mudrick, p. 306; Stolley, p. 55; Brian Moore, "Too Much Hocus in the Pocus," *Book Week*, 9 January 1966, p. 4.

2. W.W. Robson, *Modern English Literature* (London, Oxford, and New York: Oxford University Press, 1970), p. 140; Mudrick, p. 307.

3. Oates, p. 1; Angus Wilson, "Fowles's Foul Fantasy," *The Critic* (August-September 1966), p. 51; Moore, p. 4; Bernard Bergonzi, *The Situation of the Novel* (Pittsburgh: University of Pittsburgh, c. 1971), pp. 75-76.

4. Penelope Mortimer, "Into the Noosphere." *New Statesman*, 6 May 1966, p. 659.

5. Boston, p. 2.

6. Scholes, p. 6.

7. Fowles, "Guide to a Man-Made Planet," p. 8.

8. Scholes, p. 6.

9. Eric Ambler, *Epitaph for a Spy* (New York: Bantam, [1938] 1953), p. 134.

10. John Fowles, "Unasked," *Transatlantic Review* 16 (Summer 1964): 36-37.

11. Scholes, p. 8.

12. Ibid., p. 12.

13. Boston, p. 2.

14. Bergonzi, p. 75.

4
Iron Law and Golden Age

The French Lieutenant's Woman moves from the electrical suddenness of postwar Europe depicted in *The Magus* to the flushed pomposities of Victorian England. But Fowles's decision to set his third novel a century in the past marks no retreat. No moral escapism weakens Fowles's latest book; humanity has not worn thin, love is still worth working for, the ordinary is still wonderful for simply existing. *The French Lieutenant's Woman* contains as many cosmopolitan innovations as *The Magus*. But because it visits another era, not another country, these innovations are more temporal than spatial.

Most of the action takes place in Lyme Regis (Dorset), a vacation resort of some 3,000 inhabitants on the south-central coast of England. A flange of blue lias clay and limestone reaching down from Yorkshire forms its bedrock. The fossils unearthed there have made Lyme Regis a treasure trove for geologists, particularly in the nineteenth century, when Mary Anning's Old Fossil Shop and the geological findings of Lyell brought the scientific minded to town. Lyme's leading landmark, though, a curved stone pier called the Cobb, has nothing to do with science. Dating from the Middle Ages, it once served as a busy center for shipbuilding and trade. But increases in both shipbuilding and the size of merchant ships made the Cobb obsolete by the eighteenth century. In 1867, the time setting of *The French Lieutenant's Woman,* it was used chiefly for fishing smacks and pleasure crafts. These sailing vessels come into view several times during the narrative. Like them, other local details dot the action; the action begins on the Cobb, and Charles Smithson, the main male character, sometimes buys fossils from Miss Anning.

The England arching above Lyme shared little of the town's relaxed holiday mood. British capitalism came of age between 1850-75, with English trade booming beyond expectation both at home and abroad. This commercial explosion ignited large-scale changes outside the realm of trade. E. Royston Pike summarizes the change by nothing how Great Britain became, in these twenty-five years, "the world's workshop, the world's carrier, the world's clearing house, the world's banker, and a good deal else." This "good deal else" refers to "great advances in political representation, public education, sanitary improvements, the provision of housing accommodation, the emancipation of women, and social matters generally."[2] Yet, Pike reminds us, this picture was clouded. Disease, malnutrition, and the exploitation of labor were everyday realities. Waterways were fouled, food was adulterated, familes lived over their cesspools, and both women and children worked long hours in unsanitary conditions.

1867 reflects this clouded social picture. The year saw the discovery of diamonds in South Africa, the publication of *Das Kapital,* the passage of the Second Reform Bill, the formation of the Dominion of Canada, and the quelling of nationalistic risings in Ireland. But Fowles does not measure the year by these cultural landmarks alone. The private weighs as heavily as the public; and since error is a human attribute, the failures of 1867 play the same part in forming the year's character as do the successes. If 1867 saw important triumphs, it also set into motion the tragic love life of Fowles's literary hero and fellow Dorsetman, Thomas Hardy. And just to show that what did not happen can count as much for Fowles as historical fact, he dates the start of female emancipation in England 30 March 1867, when Parliament first debated but then voted down woman's suffrage.

These documentary materials do not make *The French Lieutenant's Woman* an historical novel; indeed, Fowles decries the label, *historical novel,* for his book.[3] He makes Victorian England look strange and new. His energy, thirst for knowledge, and love of extravagance are, in fact, more Elizabethan than Victorian. John Fowles has many narrative gifts, and he draws on most of them in his latest novel. He fuses the journalist's sharp view of surfaces with the philosopher's insight into first principles. What emerges triumphantly is a philosophy, a critical portrait of an age, and a crackling good yarn. "An outlandish achievement!"[4] peals Joyce Carol Oates. No mere survey, the book describes Victorian life, spoofs the age's shortcomings, and, yes, salutes its greatness. But where does *The French Lieutenant's Woman* get its power and scope? its analytical force and lyrical splendor? How does it avoid showing its seams and stitching? The truth is that *The French Lieutenant's Woman* belongs to a new category of prose fiction. Breaking with today's aesthetic norms, it carries a fiction into the fields of comparative cultural history and sociology.

This inclusiveness gives the novel the look of inventing itself as it goes along. Just as the last Beatle albums, with their controversial dust jackets, cut-outs, and picture booklets, offer more than music, *The French Lieutenant's Woman* relies on superliterary effects. Besides starting with an epigraph, it posts one or more epigraphs at the head of each of its sixty-one chapters. In keeping with its scholarly bent, it has an Acknowledgements page, and it resorts freely to both footnotes and learned allusions. Its comic tone accounts for the playful references to notable figures of 1867-1967 that stipple its surface and for Fowles's inserting himself twice in the action. These walk-ons, his halting the action to make fun of himself making fun of Henry James, the treatises on fictional technique, the tours through Victorian London, and the novel's excursions into etymology all recall the Shakespearean metaphor governing *The Magus*: "All the world's a stage." *The French Lieutenant's Woman* is a Victorian vaudeville show, a magical mystery tour through Victorian England, and Fowles is the impressario-guide. Whether he is describing a love scene or analyzing a Tennyson lyric, his show holds together. His ongoing dramas of social change, evolution, and the mutability of life everywhere keep this solidity from clotting into arbitrariness or a disgorging of facts. The historical perspective built into the Victorian storytelling mode provides still more freshness and freedom, contrary to Henry James's disclaimers against authorial omniscience.

But the matching of a Victorian setting to a Victorian idiom is a topic that deserves special attention.

I

Edward T. Chase praises the novel's fine balance of inclusiveness and execution in his *New Republic* review: "Fowles manages to encompass sophisticated commentary about the novel form with historical and philosophical insights, all so dextrously handled as to scarcely impede the narrative."[5] Our job now is to find why a narrative mode as stale as the author-centered Victorian novel can promote so much dash and depth. To expedite the job, let us talk first about the Godlike freedom Victorian novelists arrogated to themselves as taletellers. The voice of *The French Lieutenant's Woman* is the same as that of a novel by Dickens, George

Eliot, or Trollope. First, Fowles adopts both the fussy, formalized syntax and vocabulary of novelists of a century ago: his characters do not use contractions when they speak; a basement kitchen is a "Stygian domain"; a virgin has "a profound ignorance of the reality of copulation." This idiom lends power to the novelist's all-knowing, decreeing stance. Fowles faces his reader directly. He not only tells the story; he breaks in at will in order to criticize or interpret it; he worries his ideas with a Victorian doggedness. *The French Lieutenant's Woman* is not a restrained book. Its busy, thickly worked surface imparts the strong, hard colors of Victorian England. But Fowles's humor and moral relativism prevent his ideas from becoming dogmatic pronouncements. Grinning through his stiff, flounced exterior, he enjoys his freedom. He will arrow across human experience with all the wisdom and aplomb of a god. Not only will he analyze character and fill in historical background; but he also takes the privilege of discussing a character's afterlife—her being barred from heaven and then falling to the "tropical abode" "where her real master waited."

This omniscience and omnipotence also includes the lordly refusal to divulge all he knows or to seek explanations wherever he turns. He respects his characters too much—their freedom and privacy—to account for all their actions. Yet even when he resists telling all, he reminds us—often with a Godlike anachronism— that he knows more than he is telling: "Why Mrs. Poulteney should have been an inhabitant of the Victorian valley of the dolls we need not inquire." Fowles rings many witty changes on the omniscient author's privilege to impart or withhold information. His walking into the novel stems from his ongoing self-concept of all-powerful narrator. Why limit his omnipotence to storytelling? His addressing the sleeping face of a character in a railroad coach, "What the devil am I going to do with you?" joins narrator to narration in a comic stroke that baffles aesthetic dogma. The stroke also reminds the reader, first, that he is reading a book and, next, that the Victorian storytelling mode colors and infiltrates any moral judgments the book generates.

Acting as a countercheck, Fowles's coy self-rebukes warn the reader of the fallibility of the Godlike narrator of Victorian fiction; we are to guard against wholesale acceptance of his ideas and arguments. What is more, his self-rebukes help form a working partnership, a democratic framework of communication, between reader and writer. Thus Fowles chides himself for using too many exclamation points. Leaping brazenly ahead in time, he says in Chapter Five that one of his characters, Ernestina Freeman, died the same day Hitler invaded Poland in 1939. In Chapter Forty-four, he lets on that Charles Smithson, twelve years her senior, survived her by ten years. Then, rather than correcting this implausibility, he reproves himself for it and hops to another topic. Playful moments like these add bounce to the book; besides giving its morality a human reference, they make *The French Lieutenant's Woman* a novel-in-the-making rather than a disguised sermon. The context for all this, Fowles keeps reminding us, is literary. In the second chapter, two characters walk by the steps Louisa Musgrove fell down in Jane Austen's *Persuasion*; a butler has the same name, that is, Benson, as the Feverels' butler in Meredith's novel *The Ordeal of Richard Feverel*; during a passage of Hawthornesque ambiguity, the self-styled "scarlet woman of Lyme" pricks her finger on a hawthorn bush. Finally, Fowles extends the novel's literary reference frame beyond nineteenth-century fiction by defending Charles Smithson with a lawyer named Montague during an action set going by an angry family.

The tempo of the story depends on this kind of mixing of the old-fashioned with the new, of the cool with the florid.

Chapter Three begins with the ancient device of a character, here Charles, looking into a mirror; Ernestina, his fiancée, looks at herself in a mirror for a paragraph in Chapter Five, and Charles returns to study his "ambiguous face" in the glass again in Chapter Seven in preparation for a description of his features. Other technical devices slow the narrative when it needs analysis or reflection to subdue the vividness of dramatic event. A concert of "unrelievedly religious" music follows Charles's second tryst with Sarah Woodruff, the novel's title character and an emerging threat to Charles's future with Ernestina. While the music drones on, Charles examines both his conduct and his conscience. The device of seating him at a dreary concert has freed him to cope morally with his deepening tie to Sarah. And cope he must; his immobility and the droning music rule out distractions. His thought processes at the concert, by forcing him to take a hard look at his duties to Ernestina, both reveal his character and chart a course of future action by which his resolve may be judged.

To give his book a rich texture, Fowles varies its tempo in chapters, paragraphs, and even sentences. Different rhetorical units pull the plot forward; others digress, build background, or criticize the action. Even though changes happen quickly, the narrative moves slowly. In no hurry, Fowles avoids rushing to climaxes or conclusions. He hearkens back to the serial fiction of Dickens and Wilkie Collins by mounting suspense within a rhythm of Victorian expansiveness. The early chapters alternate between Charles and Sarah, who meet in Chapter Two but do not speak in private until Chapter Twelve. And whenever their relationship leaps forward, Fowles will shift focus. Chapters Eighteen and Twenty both show key meetings between them. Chapter Nineteen, though, introduces a new character, Dr. Grogan, with whom Charles discusses his feverish romance in Chapter Twenty-one. The focus-shifting is sometimes as amusing as it is thematic. Chapter Thirty-four ends with Charles's preparing to leave Lyme for London. The chapter ends thus: "What can an innocent country virgin know of sin? The question requires an answer. Meanwhile, Charles can get up to London on his own." The required "answer" takes the whole next chapter, a survey of illicit sexual habits in both London and rural England, with some thoughts on Hardy's sad love life and a short history of contraceptives tossed in.

The mention of Hardy calls to mind the epigraphs that head each chapter in the book. Hardy's poetry, perhaps because of its sour irony, appears often in the epigraphs. Like the posters, banners, and placards that introduce many scenes in Brecht (who is mentioned in the novel), these epigraphs, a legacy from Victorian fiction, sometimes chime, sometimes clash with the action of the coming chapter. Also as in Brecht, they may criticize the action or show a new dimension of it—a dimension that is sometimes hidden until the chapter's last paragraph. F. P. W. McDowell calls the epigraphs "organically significant":

> The chapter epigraphs from Tennyson, Darwin, Hardy, Arnold, and Marx are organically significant in the novel. All these men were in the vanguard of the age, as were Sarah and Charles; they were also limited by it . . . . Charles and Sarah are like them: imperfectly emancipated, perhaps, but further on the road to modernism than most of their contemporaries.[6]

McDowell, the novel's most perceptive reviewer, hits on Fowles's leading idea about evolution, that is all participate in change—all abet it, all hold it back. This view of evolution fits the epigraphs. What McDowell neglects is that not all the epigraphs come from Victorian writers or critics of the Victorian age. One comes from a description of Mrs. Kennedy's grief in William Manchester's best-seller, *The*

Death of a President (1967); heading the novel's last chapter is a passage from Martin Gardner's *The Ambidextrous Universe* (1967). These epigraphs, while resisting McDowell's formula, fit comfortably inside the larger picture of our century's debt to the last century.

The sheer existence of *The French Lieutenant's Woman* calls attention to this debt. Nearly seventy years after the death of Queen Victoria, up pops a Victorian novel by an important modern writer. The difference between his novel and those of a century ago comes from his knowing things about Victorian fiction that writers like Dickens did not know. *The French Lieutenant's Woman* is a very Victorian book—what Henry James would call a "great baggy monster." A long novel, especially by post-Jamesian standards, it is printed on a large page in large, Victorian-looking typeface; the generous margins framing the print add further to the book's Victorian expansiveness. Abundantly and confidently digressive, *The French Lieutenant's Woman* has an interior logic that meshes with both its Victorian page-design and narrative mode. We have already seen Fowles steering the action with the firm, fatherly hand of a Dickens or a Thackeray. He asks rhetorical questions: "Who is Sarah?" "Out of what shadows does she come?" He exclaims in mock wonder: "The color of those walls!" "Such an anticlimax!" He interjects his personal opinions: "Each age, each guilty age, builds high walls round its Versailles; and personally I hate those walls most when they are made by literature and art." McDowell relates these intrusions to the Brechtian aura cast by the chapter epigraphs. They remind the reader that the novel narrates, rather than describes, experience:

> [Fowles's] intrusions become a device to achieve effects which we regard as modern. Fowles's commentary approximates the "alienation effects" used in the modern theater, whereby the dramatist interrupts his work to dispel illusion (rather than, as

with the Victorian novelist, to intensify it) . . . . Fowles's use of Victorian aesthetic convention serves yet another purpose. It allows him to be purposefully anachronistic: to interpret the realities of the past as they bear upon the present or to interpret our present obsessions in light of their origins, or of similar preoccupations, in the past. [7]

The anachronisms McDowell mentions do make for some exciting surprises. They show that the novel is a tale to be told as well as an artifact. The moral and aesthetic standards they raise, extending through the Victorian age, touch on one of the novel's nerve centers. The question of *The French Lieutenant's Woman*'s success rests largely on the novel's Victorian medium and manner. Could Fowles have written the book in another style? How do its ideas flower better in Victorian soil than in the terrain of today?

Phyllis R. Katz's review in *Best Sellers* makes an important point about Fowles's comparative technique: "He [Fowles] makes it possible for us to see how our age has grown from that one"—[8] the Victorian. Some of the links joining Queen Victoria's age to ours are clearly visible. Others, as in English fiction's other champion of Darwinian evolution, Samuel Butler, skip a generation. Fowles does not confuse social change, which can come overnight, with evolution, the slow work of centuries. What he does do is to reveal important similarities between societies a century apart. The Victorian era has a good deal in common with Western culture since 1965. The popularity of marijuana and rock music, with its drugged, hypnotic repetitions, resembles the opium addiction, the soft-stroking languors of Swinburne and some of Tennyson, and also the flowing brushwork of pre-Raphaelite painting. The long hair, lavishness of dress, and dislike of hard, knotty poetry of wit prevailing in both ages show a preference for sensation over cognition. Today's stress upon man's primitive drives rather than his reason, found in anthropologists like Robert Ardrey and Desmond Morris, recalls, along with the resurgence of astrology, the Victorian era's blind faith in progress ("the march of mind"). And today's interest in Zen and Eastern music eases the same stress of living in a machine-ridden culture as the English fascination with Roman ritual did a century ago.

The search for values invites the comparison between the existential creed, radical individualism, and the Victorian doctrine of self-help. Fowles himself has likened existential commitment to Victorian earnestness. Personal responsibility also underlies his belief that today's nuclear threat diminishes us in the same way as the bombshell of evolution shriveled the Victorians.[9] But the Victorians were probably less haunted by loneliness and unimportance (the Nemo) than modern man. Very few of us claim the captaincy of our fate; though Hardy's "purblind Doomsters" care no more about human need than Camus's absurd universe, nobody in Wessex mistook *l'acte gratuit* for true freedom. There was no reason to get lost morally and psychologically in this way. The individual person had more force and enjoyed a higher standing in Victoria's day than he does in our collectivist times. His freedom and self-respect found its way into the age's literature. While emerging as the great age of the British novel, the second half of the nineteenth century also became the great age of the free-standing literary character. Realists like Flaubert, Tolstoy, and Dostoevsky remade the image of man. But Lawrence and Forster may be the last major English novelists to insist on the uniqueness and mystery of the human personality. The decline of the individual in our day relegates the novel of character to the past. Its stress on the supremacy of character makes *The French Lieutenant's Woman* an anachronism. Rejecting the postexistential coldness of Robbe-Grillet's "cleansed" world of impersonal objects, Fowles restores faith in the value of individual experience.

Existentialism's plea for privacy and personal choice leads Fowles to prefer societies that foster individual freedom over collectivist (or totalitarian) ones. Comparisons in the novel between the Victorian age and ours, by not always favoring us, make us take a longer look at ourselves. Fowles spends several pages (Chapter Thirty-six) spoofing Victorian sexual hypocrisy—prostitution and pornography never thrived more than during Victoria's reign. Then he punctures our smugness by showing this hypocrisy to be healthier than the frivolous sexuality of today:

> By transferring to the public imagination what they left to the private, we are the more Victorian—in the derogatory sense of the word—century, since we have, in destroying so much of the mystery, the difficulty, the aura of the forbidden, destroyed also a great deal of the pleasure.

Like sexual hypocrisy, methodicality is a patently Victorian trait that Fowles's comparative technique first spoofs and then redeems in part. Though self-important and starchy, Victorian science cleared the way for modern technology. The overdressed and overequipped scientists of the last century saw that man's future well-being depended on science, and they did not shrink from the duties their vision imposed. Though we mock these men, we owe them a great deal. If we are happier and wiser than they—and only posterity can decide this—these prolix plodders have made our wisdom and happiness possible.

The Aristos defined existence as a tug of counterforces: "We have been made to be best and happiest . . . in a tightrope situation." Fowles ascribes much of nineteenth-century England's greatness to this tension. The pull of opposing drives and needs wrung greatness out of hypocrisy, contradiction, and disagreement. More churches went up in England in the last century than in all previous centuries combined; but one out of every sixty houses in London, compared to today's ratio of one to six thousand, was a brothel:

> This tension, then—between lust and renunciation . . . lyrical surrender and tragic duty, between the sordid facts and their noble use—energizes and explains one of the age's greatest writers [viz., Hardy]; and beyond him structures the whole age itself.

This split, the novel says elsewhere, makes *Dr. Jekyll and Mr. Hyde* the best description of the Victorian age. And the principle that explains the whole also holds for the individual parts. The pull of opposites created the rippling, living balance that underlay Hardy's writing. A letter Charles writes to Sarah describes a split being groping for wholeness in a torn world: "One half of me is inexpressibly glad to address you thus, while the other wonders how he can speak." If we have inherited nineteenth-century science, the century's hidden fears and evasions have also come down. Both for better and for worse, our age is continuous with that of Queen Victoria.

Several reviewers have called *The French Lieutenant's Woman* a Victorian novel no Victorian novelist could have written. Fowles's comparative method and use of modern psychology do put the novel beyond the creative scope of any Victorian writer. Its voice and vocabulary both seat *The French Lieutenant's Woman* stylistically in the last century and oscillate with the modern-day ideas that build its intellectual fiber. This oscillation varies the novel's tone. At times the tone is witty, detached, and gently ironical; then, without warning, it grows angry or confidential. Stylistic level changes too, to accommodate these tonal shifts. Basically, Fowles writes a strong-thewed, disciplined prose geared more to a Dickensian solidness than to either a Jane Austen-like precision or Jamesian subtlety. But he will deliberately pit his enameled prose with wordiness and awkward phraseology. Its overblown sentiment and melodrama often make *The French*

Lieutenant's Woman sound more like the florid rhetoric of Victorian magazine fiction than the solid, supple prose of serious fiction. While its treacly, self-embedded sentences have mass, they lack point and force; while they wallow in a Dickensian whimsy and theatricality, they lack Dickensian terror. What makes all this so amazing is that the stylistic clutter supports the weight of a major novel.

First, its wooden prolixity gives it a curious suddenness. By ignoring, distorting, or overshooting an object, Fowles reveals while he conceals. Together with the other Victorian norms underlying the novel, style fosters a mood of rigidity and restraint in *The French Lieutenant's Woman.* This heavy, ornate controlling mechanism makes any ruffles on the richly globed surface of the action, however slight, stand out vividly. In a restrained atmosphere, the smallest deviation becomes wildly suggestive; the unusual becomes the forbidden. So when the book's one sexual encounter takes place, it is so explosive it nearly blows the top of your head off. Verbal irony also criticizes while it describes in Fowles's references to the twentieth century. These references shock the reader for springing out of a colonnade of stately Victorian syntax. It is as if a Yorkshireman from *Wuthering Heights* tried to explain the unleashing of wild passion to a member of the Pickwick Club. References to television, jet planes, and the Gestapo shatter the novel's Victorian patina and repose. They also jounce the reader into viewing the action historically. Fowles guides us back and forth in time in order to present the action from strange angles and to apply fresh standards of judgment. A young maidservant, we are told, is the prettiest, liveliest, and least selfish of the three young women featured in the novel; Fowles adds that her twenty-two-year-old great-great-granddaughter is a famous film actress today. This observation not only validates the previous one; it also posits a time-tested standard of beauty and perhaps goodness that gauges the conduct of the characters.

Though style and authorial intrusion both criticize the action, Fowles does not let his views color motive and choice. He comments on the action, but he does not control it. The book's most famous digression, a lecture on novel-writing that takes up all of Chapter Thirteen, stresses the importance of free characters in fiction. The chapter begins coyly with Fowles teasing the reader: "These characters I create never existed outside my own mind"; he invites different interpretations for the novel: "Perhaps I am writing a transposed autobiography . . . perhaps Charles is myself disguised." Then he discusses the stance of the novelist. Though the Victorian novelist stood next to God, he could not usurp all the vitality of his novel; fictional worlds must be treated as living organisms, not as machines. And vitality comes only from freedom. Characters must take on lives of their own, regardless of plot or authorial will: "A genuinely created world must be independent of its creator; a planned world (a world that reveals its planning) is a dead world. It is only when our characters and events disobey us that they begin to live." Narrative art depends less on point of view than on the author's surrendering control and authority. This surrender makes fiction writing more difficult, but it stimulates the flow of oxygen and blood. Any novelist, regardless of method, is a Godlike manipulator. But he will not usurp his characters' choices. Rather, he will glory when characters act on their own: "When Charles left Sarah . . . I ordered him to walk straight back to Lyme Regis. But he did not." McDowell shows how this brake on the novelist's freedom squares with Fowles's theology. Divine nonintervention, says *The Aristos*, serves individual freedom. The god who never reveals himself puts the burdens of self-responsibility and self-being right where they belong—on the shoulders of each person:

The modern omniscient author will be godlike on the side of freedom rather than of authority, and will be unable to prevent his characters from expanding as their inner beings dictate. [10]

II

Charles Smithson is a character whose will works independently of his author's. Fowles fixes him squarely in his age, endows him with a personality, gives him a difficult choice, and then shows that choice reordering his life in unexpected ways. In each phase of his self-discovery, Charles surprises. He is both a wealthy Victorian gentleman, aware of social privilege, and an existential hero-in-the-making, sloughing his privileges in order to overcome and create himself anew. He says at the outset, "That's the trouble with provincial life. Everyone knows everyone and there is no mystery. No romance." As in *The Magus,* though, the familiar shows a strange side. Like Nicholas Urfe, Charles moves from complacency to doubt, from the known to the undiscovered, and from safety to danger. The end of the book shows him disinherited, friendless, and cut off from the woman he loves. Nor does he have outlets or diversions. People today look for faster ways to do things; our problem is finding the time to do all we want. Victorian man, especially the Victorian gentleman, did not feel this crowding and rush. Less besieged by stimuli, he had more than enough time for all he wanted to do. Like Frederick Clegg in *The Collector,* Charles lacks the polarity of work routine. He is standing still in a fast-moving age. What is more, though he dislikes his immobility, he lacks the spark and forward drive to change. His "negative but comfortable English soul" is a bland mix of "one part irony to one part convention."

Charles's preferences typify the Victorian man of leisure; he likes foreign travel, intellectual dabbling, superficial rela-

tionships, and physical comfort. His passion for social appearance makes him slavishly conventional. Keeping up appearances are to Charles what material possession and fiction were
to Clegg and Urfe. Like Clegg's drive to own beauty and
Urfe's drive to make every challenge an aesthetic sensation,
Charles has *his* private escapist fantasy—the need to regulate
his conduct by what people think. This conformity has not
prepared him well for hazard, change, and emotional stress.
At thirty-two, he has asked life many questions but has not
hungered for answers. Tired of using foreign travel as a mar-
riage-substitute, he feels that life has passed him by. But he
does not enjoy the bystander's safety and detachment. Social
change and a growing body of scientific method are both
closing in on him. A favorite of mothers with marriageable
daughters, he has, until recently, avoided matrimonial traps.
Now, his growing obsession with Sarah Woodruff and the
guilt he feels over dishonoring his engagement to Ernestina
rasp his nerves. Though his front name is that of both Victorian England's most famous scientist and novelist, he lacks the
perseverance and inventive force to become a Darwin or a
Dickens: "Laziness was, I am afraid, Charles's distinguishing
trait." Conversely, he lacks the spontaneity, physical strength,
and self-assurance to play the rake.

Bright enough to spot the flaws in British society and
honest enough to be appalled by them, Charles has a rebellious streak. Yet his rebellion, before he meets Sarah, has
little force. Whereas Sarah's promise of renewal makes her
"the woman who was the door," he is called "the man without
the key." He cannot unlock her mystery, and his failure—like
that of Joyce's Leopold Bloom, who forgets his house key in
Ulysses—is strongly sexual. He travels with open, critical eyes;
he supports the doctrine of evolution; he cavils against British
narrowness. He dabbles in science, especially paleontology;
for a hobby, he collects marine fossils, especially the petrified

sea urchins called *tests*. This hobby is strangely revealing. His life-style puts him in danger of hardening into a fossil himself; he is even called "one of life's victims . . . a potential turned into a fossil." Unformed and unready, Charles needs training—but not as a scientist or collector. Only art can make him whole—by showing him the sacredness of life, by teaching him about human relationships, and by discouraging him from shaping life to a logical system or formula:

> The specific value of art for man is that it is closer to reality than science; that it is not dominated, as science must be, by logic and reason; that it is therefore essentially a liberating activity while science—for excellent and necessary causes—is a constricting one. Finally . . . it is the best, because richest, most complex and most easily comprehensible, medium of communication between human beings (*The Aristos*).

Science leads Charles to Sarah. One day while searching for fossils of extinct species, he chances upon her, a new species, and "the whole Victorian age was lost." Charles sees in Sarah a sexual fulfillment close to Lawrence's star-polarity ideal in *Women in Love:* "an intimacy of thought and feeling hitherto unimaginable to him in the context of a relationship with a woman." This intimacy overwhelms him. But, even though he only offers Ernestina a playful, patronizing warmth, he resists Sarah. Ian Watt has summarized a good part of Charles's inability to welcome Sarah:

> In the struggle between the old and new species, Charles wants to side with the new; but he learns to his cost that he has relied too much on the old "law of gravity" which assumed that "fallen women must continue falling." [11]

Watt is right; Charles's reaction to Sarah is not just sexual or moral. Charles responds to her with the force of his whole personality, including the conditioning of his crotchety era.

Fowles has good reason to call him "a man struggling to overcome history." He overcomes a great deal to keep his love
affair with Sarah alive. And he does act in a manly, decent
way more than once. He will not toady his wealthy bachelor
uncle, a Wiltshire baronet, to inherit the uncle's title and
estate. He walks out of a London brothel, where some friends
had taken him, if only to hire a Cockney streetwalker less than
an hour later.

That he leaves the streetwalker without having sex with
her derives from Fowles's sexual ethic. Like that of Lawrence,
Fowles's belief in the redemptive force of sexual love has a
religious drive. He also follows Lawrence in equating the
sexual with the religious impulse. This equation he works brilliantly into the narrative economy of *The French Lieutenant's
Woman.* The novel's form forbids Charles's having sex with
anybody in the novel but Sarah. The shock of this event
propels Charles to a nearby church, where he sees Sarah's face
in place of Jesus' on the rough wood of the cross. But Charles
wastes his vision. *The Aristos* called Christianity "badly
flawed" because it has caged Jesus; the belief that Christ can
only be reached through dogma and ritual divides man from
God. In a moment of surpassing intensity, Charles fuses erotic
joy, emotional growth, and self-understanding within a
religious frame. The crucifix topped by Sarah's face shows
Charles the purpose of Christianity: "to bring about a world in
which the hanging man could be descended, could be seen . . .
with . . . the smiling peace of a victory brought about by, and
in, living men and women." The risen Christ, not the dead
man or the church-caged God, embodies the Christian imperative. Man's deepest needs can be filled by the divine legacy of
the Holy Ghost, or spirit of love, that pulsates through all.
What this epiphany means is the attainment of self-discovery
and self-acceptance through union with the social outcast,
Sarah. Charles chooses Sarah on an intensely personal basis.

That he chooses freely while praying by himself makes his choice a function of mystical communion—the alone with the alone. The choice is unconditioned by propriety, duty, or material gain. By electing to marry Sarah, he does not choose *for* life so much as choosing life itself. The choice is magnetic; his physical and mystical conjunction with the outcast does not run its course until he becomes an outcast himself.

By setting Charles's golden moment in a church (Saint Mary's in Exeter), Fowles gives Charles a glow found in neither Clegg nor Urfe. Charles Smithson is Fowles's most likeable male character, and his revelation in Chapter Forty-eight sparks much of his warmth. It also sets him a challenge more exacting than any undergone by Clegg or Urfe. Charles's visit to Exeter both creates and defines him. Everything that goes before it leads up to it; everything that follows leads away. Charles is too deeply dyed by his era to realize his vision. His liberation is incomplete, and it feels more like chastisement than joyful release. First, he does not go right back to Sarah after leaving Saint Mary's Church; he feels morally bound to break his engagement with Ernestina before undertaking another. He writes Sarah a letter instead of telling her in person about his duty to Ernestina; finally, he gives the letter to a servant rather than taking it himself. A modern-day lover, that is, one whose emotions have been colored by existentalism, would not waste a moment before joining his beloved.

But another, more subtle, explanation for these mistakes comes to mind. It grows out of a belief that haunts all of Fowles—"the black paradox at the heart of the human condition" that we cannot enjoy what we have, that to slake desire is to kill desire.[12] Charles keeps mystery and yearning aglow by taking a roundabout course back to Sarah. For he not only holds his painful interview with Ernestina *before* attempting to see Sarah again but he also uses the trip to Lyme to have speech with his secular father-confessor, Dr. Grogan. Fowles never explains this dawdling. He does not have to. *The French Lieutenant's Woman* understates, surmises, and even hides meaning as often as it analyzes and interprets. Perhaps Charles wanted to get lost on his way back to Sarah. His snail-like moral fastidiousness and his flight into the dark, enclosing warmth of the church both war against a close relation grounded in sex. Also, his delays and misjudgments give him a purpose he never had before. He spends the next two years searching for Sarah, both in England and the United States. The telegram announcing her discovery ends the only sustained effort of his life—an effort, like that of Urfe, that consists largely of waiting.

Charles exists both in Victorian England and all time. Evolving from nineteenth- to twentieth-century man in 1867-69, he leads his century by more than thirty years. Evolving in a niggardly, crabwise way, instead of darting forward, he reflects all of us. Charles admires evolution as an idea. His prospective father-in-law, Mr. Ernest Freeman, makes him test the Darwinian principle that survival depends on adaptation when he offers him a partnership in his huge store. In a scene that must have occurred hundreds of times in the last century, the crafty "commercial giant" corners the gentleman whose title he has bought for his daughter. The scene conveys the push-pull rhythm that energizes all upheaval. Charles resists Mr. Freeman's offer because a gentleman does not work. Belonging to a class that knows nothing of work, he is both untrained and unfit for work. His resisting a job reflects an inability to shake free from social class and to change with the times. Failing to practice the Darwinian preachment of survival through adaptation, he retards evolution. Idler, "born amateur," and "victim of evolution," he carries the print of a dying social class.

But at least he knows that his life's purpose has nothing

to do with Mr. Freeman's great store on Oxford Street. His refusal to work proclaims his freedom. The Victorian gentleman class that hems him in formed "a self-questioning ethical elite" that rejected material possession as life's chief value. Human survival depends on the existence of nonmaterialist minorities like this, and most ages, happily, have provided subcultures to answer the call. Charles's refusal of a job may have pinned him hopelessly to a dying tradition, but it also vindicates free choice and nonacquisitiveness as functions of being human. So important is this flight from ownership that Fowles highlights it in the novel's epigraph, from Marx's *Zur Judenfrage:* "Every emancipation is a restoration of the human world and of human relationships to man himself."

A name less famous than Darwin's or Dickens's but which extends just as powerfully from the last century is that of James Smithson, donor of the Smithsonian Institute in Washington, D.C. Ian Watt notes two ways in which Fowles's character resembles him: "He is destined to go to America and he expects to inherit a fortune and baronetcy."[13] One of Charles's greatest shocks comes when his wealthy sixty-seven-year-old bachelor uncle announces his forthcoming marriage. Charles's exclusion from a title and dimmed financial outlook both foreshadow his self-imposed exile from England after breaking with Ernestina. Born in France and to die in Italy, James Smithson shares some of his namesake's background of foreign travel. Though, unlike Charles, he never crossed the Atlantic, he did bequeath his fortune to the United States. This bequest, coming at the expense of a nephew, echoes in the novel, as do Smithson's noble birth—his father was a duke—and scientific bent. But Charles's Darwinism and fossil collection pale before his eponym's work in chemistry and mineralogy; Smithsonite, a carbonate of zinc ($ZnCO_3$), is named in Smithson's honor. The loudest echo, though, booming from the gap between Charles and his real-life counterpart sounds the theme of evolution. Though Charles's social and scientific credentials fall short of Sir James Smithson's, they still emit hope. Charles's isolation and lostness at the end form the existential climate where free, creative acts occur. Any judgment of Charles's worth goes beyond the frontiers of the novel. But the force generated by Sir James Smithson also shatters fixed bounds. His dates (1765-1829) and the efflorescence of museums in the nineteenth century make him as much of a transitional man as Charles.

A more discernible transition is achieved by Sarah Woodruff, the book's title character, figure of mystery, and handmaid of evolution. Hazard has both blessed and cursed Sarah. Victorian England was an age of great men; Sarah shows that it was also an age of great women, though nobody bothered to look. Even Dickens has drawn Fowles's fire for his "almost complete inability to invent intelligent, independent, women."[14] Any society reveals itself in action. What men and women say and do together helps determine social health for Fowles: "The male and the female are the two most powerful biological principles; and their smooth interaction in society is one of the chief signs of social health" (*The Aristos*). Victorian England enjoyed no such health because Victorian woman lacked force. In a passage that foreshadows Sarah's plight in *The French Lieutenant's Woman, The Aristos* adds the biological and sociological cost of depriving women of all but the lowest means of earning money:

> Adam is stasis, or conservatism; Eve is kinesis, or progress. Adam societies are the ones in which the man and the father, male gods, exact strict obedience to established institutions and norms of behavior . . . . The Victorian is a typical such period. Eve societies . . . encourage innovation and experiment . . . . The Renaissance and our own are typical such ages.

Any society takes its life from social relationships. The only power a woman has in a personal tie with a man is the power to withhold sex. This power had little force in Victorian England, because a gentleman did not expect extramarital sex outside the brothel. Sarah cannot even hope for a close personal tie with a man. Like Hardy's Eustacia Vye, in *Return of the Native,* another vivid heroine offered a job reading to an elderly lady, she enters the book in sharp relief to both nature and society. Also like Eustacia, her fortunes depend largely on an undelivered letter. Sarah is passionate and wild, the only tragic figure in the book; "Poor Tragedy," in fact, is one of her nicknames. Her passion and impulse shame Charles, making his anxiety over social appearances look small and cheap. "Poor Tragedy" describes her environment as well as it does her; her lack of power, besides thwarting her, becomes society's, even posterity's loss.

In a 1970 essay, "My Recollections of Kafka," Fowles notes Kafka's obsessions. But "the insoluble mysteries of existence, the futility of society, the paranoiac sense of victimization" he finds in Kafka also run through his own work. (He admits having been influenced by Kafka.)[15] Sarah finds both her physical surroundings and the spirit of her age as hostile as Miranda did in *The Collector.* She is checked wherever she turns. Her strong, tragic face counts against her in an age favoring shy, demure looks in women. What people find most striking in her face are her lancing, shooting eyes. Sarah's eyes look *through* rather than *at* people; one character talks about the danger of looking into them; another calls them "drowning eyes," eyes a man could drown in. This penetration goes against the prevailing social nostrum favoring submissiveness in women. Sarah is one of those rare "Adam women" *The Aristos* mentions, a fusion of female gentleness and male analytical power. She is also a Darwinian heroine, disproving the Linnean maxim, *nulla species nova,* no new species can come into being. But her milieu resists her. If a new species enters the world, says Darwin, older ones have to move aside. Because nobody moves aside to make room for Sarah, she becomes "the perfect victim of a caste society." Her father went mad after his farm failed, and after his death in Dorchester Asylum, she had to fend for herself. But she has had nowhere in which to grow. (Her grief comes logically from the collision of her quintessential womanhood and her harsh masculine age.) But, as has been seen, her grief and loss do not stop with her. An anachronism, she proves the bitter truth that humankind can fight evolution, its best friend: "She appeared inescapably doomed to the one fate nature had so clearly spent many millions of years in evolving her to avoid: spinsterhood."

Her attempt to make sense of her hostile surroundings links her again to Miranda Grey. But, curiously, her situation traces just as clear a descent from Nicholas Urfe. To begin with, Sarah's alleged descent from Sir Francis Drake parallels Urfe's disputed blood tie with the seventeenth-century writer, Honoré D'Urfé. The possibility that Sarah (along with Thomas Hardy) was born exactly three hundred years after Drake, whose birth date is usually given as 1540; her appearing first near a body of water that figured in England's war against the Armada; her modest rural beginnings; the power she gains to steer several lives—these links with the great Elizabethan ship's navigator and commander limn a line of heredity from Drake as thematic as that between D'Urfé and Urfe in *The Magus*. Sarah also goes to work as a governess for the same reason that Urfe becomes a teacher—for want of a better opportunity. She thus foreshadows historically and stems intellectually from Amis's Lucky Jim Dixon, Osborne's Jimmy Porter, and Wain's Charles Lumley (*Hurry on Down*). These characters all come from the 1950s, when *The Magus* takes place. Like Sarah, each is an educated provincial whose origins limit his social mobility but whose temperament and training make him unfit for the provinces. Again like Sarah, each of these men gets the chance to marry above his social station.

But none of them knows the frustration of being a governess—caring for other women's children and being reminded by them every day that you will probably never have children of your own. Some of this frustration gets into the books's first picture of Sarah in Chapter One. This striking picture shows Sarah standing at the end of the Cobb on an "incisively sharp and blustery" March morning in 1867. Fowles builds a drama around her lonely vigil. Her worn black coat, which looks like a man's, contrasts her with Ernestina and Charles, "people of very superior taste as regards their outward appearance," who are also out on the Cobb. Sarah is motionless and nondescript; she is referred to as "it," "the figure," and "a living memorial to the drowned, a figure from myth." Once mistaken for a fisherman, she looks more like a monument than a person. The book's finale changes all this. No longer does she withstand sharp blustery winds. The tightly drawn-back hair of Chapter One flows richly, almost to her waist. She looks two years younger rather than two years older than she did since Charles last saw her. Wearing the bright undulating colors of the New Woman in place of her sullen fisherman's coat, she emerges "blossomed, realized, winged from the back pupa" of Chapter One.

But why? What causes this spectacular change? What price does she pay for it? And, since our actions always touch other, how does the change affect those around her?

The Old Testament origins of her first name imply a remorseless *Realpolitik*. Everything has a price; Sarah's rebirth, like that of Charles, both follows birth-pangs and casts a death-like shadow. In line with her Biblical namesake, Sarah renews herself through motherhood; part of her splendor at the end comes from her having her baby daughter at her side. The Biblical parallel need not be dropped. Her Old Testament faith and strength turn out to be her greatest assets, promoting her own and other people's growth. Her youth, independence, and the shrewdness with which she picks her opportunities, on the other hand, make her a poor example of a resigned Old Testament mother. Sarah serves renewal actively. Her Hardyesque last name implies the same life-giving qualities as her first; Woodruff is the name of an herb sometimes called *Blood Cup* and *Kiss-Me-Quick* in Dorset. Its more common name, *hay-plant,* comes from the sweet, haylike smell it gives off while drying. This phenomenon re-flects Fowles's fascination with the organic interplay in the universe of life and death, birth and decay; for the dried woodruff petals, besides exhaling fragrance, make delicious tea. That the herb cures headache, dispels melancholy, and opens the liver and gall bladder touches on Sarah's skill as a healer; she met and grew close to Varguennes, a French naval officer, while nursing him back to health after a shipwreck near Lyme Bay. The plant's Old English name, finally, *Wuderofe,* implies "roving, creeping, spreading," [16] three traits that refer to the influence Sarah gains on her luckier and wealthier counterparts.

Now the practice of using a book's outward appearance as a critical tool is dangerous. Yet the novel's dust-jacket portrait of the artist's wife, Mary Adams, who, by a fantastic coincidence, was born only a few miles from Sarah's fictional birthplace, carries uncannily into the text. This portrait, which also appears on the endpapers of the novel's British (Jonathan Cape) edition, shows Sarah gazing out to sea as in Chapter One, her hooded tragic eyes dominating the scene. The total effect is one of inner strength. The dark hair pulled back from the vaulting forehead and the proud, heavy eye-brows combine with her firmly blocked-in nose and mouth to give an impression of womanly resolve. The portrait helps validate her superiority over the townsfolk who mock, restrain, and ostracize her. A free spirit, she is delicate, tough-minded, and physically well made.

The following passage gives another reason for her superiority:

> Saras **was** intelligent, but her real intelligence belonged to a rare kind . . . . It was not in the least analytical or probelm-solving . . . . It was rather an uncanny . . . . ability to classify other people's worth: to understand them, in the fullest sense of the word.

Fowles later locates "her essence" in "understanding and emotion." Impulse, intuition, and passion distinguish her. She seems to enjoy children more than grown-ups; her love for Charles governs her conduct; she speaks "directly" of Christ's suffering even though she has no formal religious belief. Her solitary walks in the Undercliff, a chasm-filled preserve, recall Christ's prowling around the desert by himself. The luxuriance of this wild cliff meadow makes it Sarah's natural milieu. Structurally, the Undercliff's green recesses and leafy tunnels form a nice vegetable contrast to the sea, universal symbol of life, where Sarah enters the book. Yet these clefts and gorges have a sharper Freudian reference than Lyme Bay. Vegetable life throngs the Undercliff. The bracken grows seven or eight feet high; flowers bloom a month earlier there than anywhere else in the neighborhood. Fowles gives this mad luxuriance a human basis. Staying within his Freudian frame, he endows the Undercliff with mystery and danger. Its soil has never been tilled; unfriendly to human purpose, it is now uninhabited; it has spots "where a man with a broken leg could shout all week and not be heard."

This fertility, wildness, and danger make it right that Sarah and Charles's relationship both starts and then flourishes in the Undercliff; except for the scene in Exeter, the Undercliff is where Sarah and Charles have their intensest moments. In Chapter Ten, the first time he sees her alone, she is sleeping on a grassy slope. His accidental awakening of her calls to mind the sleeping beauty motif that runs through so much of D. H. Lawrence. For Charles is also awakened here. In fact, his waking up hits us more explosively than hers. Just before Charles happens upon her sleeping figure, Fowles moves from his customary omniscience to Charles's point of view. The impact gained by this shift in stance is tremendous. We become aware of Sarah's beauty together with Charles. Shrewdly, Fowles makes the driving pulse of this awakening a sensory impression—Sarah's beautiful hair. Her hair in Chapter One, again, was pulled back and tucked under her collar. Here, in Chapter Ten, its waving richness becomes continuous with the teeming undergrowth. This continuity sets into motion the emergence of her hair as a sexual symbol. After its electrifying appearance in the Undercliff, Sarah's hair is not fully displayed until Exeter, where Sarah and Charles make love. Sarah quickly engineers a sexual context for this meeting by spreading her "ravishingly alive" hair on a dark green shawl, expressly bought for the occasion. She thus re-creates for Charles's benefit the scene in the Undercliff where he found her asleep. And her imaginative re-creation drives home. On the next page, Charles feels "a prisoner in a green field, a hawk rising." As soon as Sarah's shawl drops from her shoulders, undulating her hair against her thin flannel nightgown, he carries her into the bedroom. The hair symbolism reaches its logical development in Sarah's last appearance in the book. Here, her daughter by her side, Sarah's hair dips triumphantly to her waist. The sexual drama has run its biological and symbolic course. The sexless "monument" of Chapter One has become a sexual force amid thronging green life and enjoys the crowning reward of sex— parenthood. The colorful family tableau comprising mother, father, and child squares the symbolic account.

But it leaves other accounts unsettled, and it is not the last scene in the book. What the tableau leaves out, specifically, is Sarah's mystery. To discuss Sarah and leave out her mystery is not to discuss her at all. Guy Davenport says about her, "Her essence is in the fact that she can't be understood."[17] This enigma puts her beyond formulas and definitions. But it does not put her beyond discussion. All her actions make sense as expressions of a unique personality trapped inside a unique social milieu. In his summary of Sarah's intelligence, quoted above, Fowles, choosing his words carefully, mentioned her "ability to classify other people's worth." Elsewhere he says she was "born with a computer in her heart." Sarah shares the Victorian mania for categories and labels. Although conceptless, she reverts to paradigms and systems. Ruled by feeling, she understands the life of the heart, and she can manipulate the feelings of others. Her shrewdness and calculation show through in the effect she has on others. Considering her poverty, her empty future, and the prevailing belief in Lyme that her broken love affair with Varguennes, the decamped French Lieutenant, has wrecked her mind, this impact is amazing.

The person hit hardest by the impact is Charles. Miss Oates's review of *The French Lieutenant's Woman* makes his choice of Sarah over Ernestina both regenerative and redemptive: Charles, says Miss Oates, "must choose between the blond, daylight civilized female and the dark, dangerous, powerfully erotic female whose love promises to destroy him but also to redeem him, to resurrect his truest self."[18] The contrast between the two women may be too sharp; yet it describes Sarah's power to renew while she destroys. Fowles is right to call her the novel's protagonist (Chapter Fifty-five). Her mystery invades and transforms several lives. It robs Ernestina of her future husband; it sends that future husband on a two-year tour of Europe and America; it lands his servant Sam Farrow, in the great London store of Ernestina's father.

Sarah changes these lives because she takes charge of her

own life.)\She usually carries her bonnet while talking to Charles in order to show off her dark, luxuriant hair. During one of their talks, she leads him up a slope, even though "a lady would have mounted behind, not ahead of him," in order to display her ankles and calves. In Exeter the pretext of an ankle injury maneuvers him into her hotel room. Sarah thus vamps him with a trick that had been tried unsuccessfully on her; when Varguennes had summoned her to *his* room in Weymouth, she "insisted he be sent for."\Both in Exeter and the Undercliff, she plays to Charles's male vanity. She confides in him, asks for his help, calls him her last resource.\ She also makes their meetings last as long as possible, and she fosters intimacy by pledging him to secrecy. Her frequent association with falls gives this scheming a Satanic aura. Her father's social and financial ruin, plunging him into madness, caused a steep drop in her fortunes; her hopes dropped again together with her reputation after her failed romance with Varguennes; she calls Varguennes, whom she loved, "the devil in the guise of a sailor"; she claims to have hurt her ankle in Exeter by falling down some stairs.\But do these Satanic echoes make her a temptress? a witch? She lures Charles to her room and bed; she plants the idea of marriage in his head.\But what is wrong about her wanting to marry the man she loves? Moreover, she does not help her chances by telling him that she gave him her virginity. She had already said, in fact, that she was Varguennes's mistress.

This unorthodoxy restores her to mystery. But she has been infusing her dark mystery, all along, with creativity. This darkness is only demonic in that it goes against the materialist ethic her society lives by.\Sarah's mystery comes from her belief in passion and instinct. Chapter One found her a nondescript blot. She continues to exude shadows and darkness; in Chapter Twelve she is called "a black figure"; in Chapter Sixteen Charles becomes aware of her as "a dark moment"; she

enters his thoughts when he stares into the dark air in Chapter
Twenty-five; a local doctor calls her predicament, "Dark
indeed. Very dark." This darkness takes on sexual force and,
therefore, its life-giving powers in the Undercliff, the novel's
seedbed for growth and abundance. None of the Undercliff's
dangers touch Sarah. She feels at home there, and promise
comes to her amid its tropical growth. Though her springtime
walks there cross her employer's wishes, they also materialize
her lover. Another pair of lovers she sees during one of her
trysts with Charles look "as greenly erotic as the April plants
they trod on." Green is the color of growing things, an
emblem of life. This lush green precivilized place, where
poachers hunt and where social arrangements are thrown
askew, endows Sarah with a healthy, lawless fertility.

But this fertility has a tragic side. Women need to exude
secrecy and mystery; men need to penetrate this female magic.
The necessary collision of these two drives can be fatal. While
obeying the rules of the sexual war, Sarah does her best to prevent casualties. Mystery is a principle of survival for her. She
says, after making love to Charles, "Do not ask me to explain
what I have done. I cannot explain it. It is not to be explained." Being and knowing exist inversely for her. She
insists that she is not to be understood, even by herself; happiness for her depends upon total opaqueness. To define the
heart's impulses too closely is to kill them; the truths that
guide her life lose their force when held up to the light. *The
French Lieutenant's Woman* is a cunning, knowledgeable
novel that discredits the knowable.

(Diagnosed as melancholic, Sarah both invites misfortune
and makes a public show of it. She will not leave Lyme, even
though her outlook there is bleak. She risks what little security
she has by walking in the Undercliff against her employer's
wishes. Then, when hazard brings Charles her way, she sends
him away, she turns down his offers of help, and she stands so

near the edge of a sharp drop that she must be restrained. She confesses an imaginary sin—sleeping with Varguennes—and begs his forgiveness. Pain is her special province. She enjoys playing the outcast; she defoliates a spray resembling "microscopic cherub's genitals." This attraction to pain and Charles's vague resemblance to Prince Albert (1819-61) bring to mind the extended mourning of Queen Victoria. This mourning made sorrow a norm of well-bred female conduct for many years, and Sarah queens it over her townsfolk in her sorrow. She is strong enough to be an individualist, even when individualism means standing alone. If she makes a show of her suppression, she cannot be blamed. Grief and frustration are all she has to distinguish herself with. A poor, classless girl, she cannot wait for Charles to make overtures. She must break all standing rules of courtship and go after him herself. But, living in an age that expects women to submit, not dominate, she cannot let her quarry know he is being stalked. Thus she bedevils, deludes, and outrages him; better a dazed lover than one who feels trapped. "All the world's a stage," said *The Magus.* Sarah's improvisations carry the metaphor into *The French Lieutenant's Woman.* They prove her a brilliant actress; the imagined and the unrevealed exist for her. She takes naturally to religion, and she ends the novel by working for an artist-poet. In a Magus-like act of self-preservation, she foists pain on herself in order to ward off the pain inflicted by others. The power she gains over others also proves her an accomplished dramatist. Her womanly mystery changes Charles's life. Furthermore, she makes several characters besides Charles act *her* script.

Fowles has grumbled about "the general human fault" of "naming things and then forgetting them."[19] No era labeled people and treated them as objects more than the Victorian. But if the people of Lyme in 1867 use the label-term, "French Lieutenant's Woman," to encompass Sarah, Fowles goes to the opposite extreme. Sarah he gives special treatment. Whereas he analyzes the others, he cloaks her in thickening layers of mystery. Charles never decides whether she is "Eve personified, all mystery and love and profundity" or "a half-scheming, half-crazed governess." The mystery fuels his imagination and keeps him on her trail for two years. It has the same Brechtian effect on the reader, forcing him to re-think the narrative. Fowles's refusal to delve into her mind makes us form our own answers; to do this we have to inter-pret personality and event with great care.

Sarah's mystery, then, accounts for much of the novel's spell. But it rests on shaky novelistic technique. The success of *The French Lieutenant's Woman* hinges on Fowles's refusal to divulge Sarah's thoughts. Nor is he timid about his silence. Rather than covering his tracks, he discusses his technique with the reader: "I no more intend to find out what was going on in her [Sarah's] mind . . . than I did on that other occa-sion" (Chapter Thirty-six). Fowles's plucky honesty does not offset the truth that he has overtaxed his doctrine of mystery as energy. All writing demands selection. But the selection must be uniform. By allowing us access into all the leading characters' minds but Sarah's, Fowles obscures the book's moral basis and disjoints narrative unity.

At a glance, Ernestina Freeman seems an inadequate love-rival to Sarah. Whereas Charles and Sarah stage their trysts in the overgrown, green-shagged Undercliff, he and Ernestina become engaged in a greenhouse, or artificial garden. Yet Fowles does not simplify the Sarah-Ernestina love rivalry into a facile dualism. Though Sarah does represent impulse and danger to Charles, Ernestina stands for more than duty, safety, and honor. She is not merely the pallid, simpering only child of an industrial pirate. When Sarah upsets her marital plans with Charles, she does not shatter a domestic calm; like any other close-felt human tie, the engagement has undercurrents of unrest and resentment. Ernestina feels ashamed of descending from trade; even though he reminds her of his "disgracefully plebian" last name, she knows that their coming marriage amounts socially to her father's buying into the upper classes. This delicate situation slides into new, more difficult straits when Uncle Bob's sudden engagement strips Charles of title and inheritance. Nobody, it turns out, has clear title to social supremacy; as in Henry James, everybody's credentials are either smirched or thin.

The apex of the Ernestina-Charles-Sarah love triangle is, of course, Charles. Ironically, he does not come up to the human level of the two women who contend for him. Ernestina outshines him as vividly as Sarah does. Her moral standards surpass his, and she asks more from life. Whereas she loves him, he is little more than amused by her. Her freshness and verve would stop her from basing a marriage on as skimpy an emotional foundation as this. But besides not loving her, he has not bothered to know her. By thinking her submissive, gentle, and predictable, he both underrates and misreads Ernestina. She has "exactly the right face for her age; that is, small-chinned, oval, delicate as a violet." Spoiled and petted, prim and fragile, she keeps a diary "in black morocco with a gold clasp" where she makes obligatory references to family, fiancé, and weather: "Wrote letter to Mama. Did not see dearest Charles. Did not go out, tho' it is very fine. Did not feel happy." What Charles overlooks and what she tries to hide are an "imperceptible hint of a Becky Sharp" (*Vanity Fair*) and the "promise of a certain buried wildness." Though powerful, this "sugar Aphrodite" hides her strong will behind a frail, fluttering exterior for convention's sake. The mask fools everybody.

When she does take it off, though, she reveals that she has inherited the iron character of her hard-driving father along with his name (Ernest). Like Charles, she attains her greatest moment in loss—when Charles comes to her in Chapter Fifty to break their engagement. Her reaction to his announcement shows sincerity, tenacity, and, because of the crashing suddenness of his words, outstanding poise. Her refusal to take refuge in moral outrage or self-pity lifts her to new heights. She outshines Charles completely in this scene. Though he acts honorably enough by breaking the engagement before contracting another, he hides the reason for his change of heart. The prepared self-debasing speech where he breaks with her lacks the vision and tenderness of her spontaneous loving reply. Honest, simple, and level in pitch, this great speech could be both the emotional and rhetorical peak of the book. The power of the writing—achieved through word choice, cadencing, and dramatic pacing—brings out the depth of her need:

> I know to you I have never been anything more than a pretty little . . . article of drawing-room furniture. I know I am innocent. I know I am spoiled. I know I am not unusual . . . . Perhaps I am just a child. But under your love and protection . . . and your education . . . I believed I should become better. I should learn to please you, I should learn to make you love me for what I had become . . . . I did not choose you because I was so innocent I could not make comparisons. But because you seemed more generous, wiser, more experienced. I remember . . . that I wrote, soon after we became engaged, that you have little faith in yourself. I have felt that. You believe yourself a failure, you think yourself despised, I know not what . . . but that is what I wished to make my real bridal present to you. Faith in yourself.

Matching these new heights of oral expression are the heights of vindictiveness Ernestina scales after Charles leaves her. Sarah in her direst moments never lashed out as angrily at Varguennes as Ernestina when, supported by her father, she makes Charles admit in writing that he dishonored his engagement to pursue a "clandestine liaison."

A character who surpasses Ernestina in naughtiness is

the pluming, swelling Lyme widow who hires Sarah as her secretary-companion, Mrs. Poulteney. Like her basement kitchen, a "Stygian domain" whose walls are "rich in arsenic," she is inconvenient, unamenable, and lethal. Though cut to the pattern of the scolding Victorian matron, she grips the reader tightly. Fowles grants her freedom rather than making fun of her, even though the freedom she craves denies the freedom of others ("She was like some plump vulture"). Her favorite pastime consists in regulating the private lives of her underpaid, overworked servants. She mines her garden with mantraps "quite powerful enough to break a man's leg" in order to keep suitors away from her maid-servants; she has Sarah watched and followed during her off-duty hours; a sadist, she will dismiss a servant for the slightest infraction. Pompous and self-righteous, she always acts predictably. Yet she is always frightening. Like Clegg in *The Collector,* she fuses the tawdry and the terrifying. As predictable as she is, nobody can afford to lower his guard around her. Fowles's ability to strike danger out of such stale melodrama betokens real inventiveness. Though a minor figure, Mrs. Poulteney makes a major impact on those around her.

A minor character less magnetic than Mrs. Poulteney but just as important thematically is Dr. Michael Grogan. Trained in Heidelberg and London, this confirmed bachelor of sixty prescribes for two of Mrs. Poulteney's servants. His importance in the novel, though, comes more from his crusty wisdom than from his medical practice alone. Several interviews he holds with Charles criticize and deepen the action rather than advancing it. A would-be scientist, Charles sees Dr. Grogan and himself as colleagues. This assessment is both right and wrong. The basis of Charles's fellowship with Dr. Grogan is Sarah, not science. Most of their talk centers on Sarah, and Dr. Grogan's spying on Sarah with his telescope in Chapter One suggests an interest that rivals Charles's. A doughty Irishman, Dr. Grogan does not let Charles sidestep the truth. In the larger picture of Fowles's developing artistry, his talks with Charles recall the confidential, confessional relationship with an older man that Urfe had with Conchis and that Clegg had with nobody; a father-figure helps the difficult process of growing up, at any level. Within the novel, Dr. Grogan underscores the evolutionary truth that all of us serve and hinder progress. His confirmed bachelorhood weighs against his championing of Darwin. Yet he is no passive hypocrite. A biologist who does not abet evolution biologically, he strengthens others for their more active evolutionary roles.

One of these others is Charles's Cockney manservant, Sam Farrow. Sam not only shows energy welling up from the lower classes, but, with a rebuke to breeding and social privilege, he also outdoes Charles both in thrift and tenderness, owing to his loving delicacy with his sweetheart Mary. Sam overcomes. By the end of the book, he has become a husband, father, homeowner, and valued employee of Mr. Freeman's Oxford Street emporium. This achievement adds to the novel's social criticism—especially Fowles's study of social change and social mobility. As Charles's servant, Sam is no Sancho Panza or Sam Weller (*The Pickwick Papers*). But then no faithful retainer could hurdle the obstacles raised by low wages and strictly controlled personal habits. Sam also adds to Fowles's doctrine of mystery. His love tie with Mary, a carter's daughter from Devon, succeeds better than either of Charles's romantic attachments. The cultural and linguistic barriers dividing Sam and Mary help their love. Given a counterpole in their masters' opposition, love came more easily to the servant class than to their masters. It also found a more beneficial milieu in the nineteenth century than it does today. Fowles does not glory in the gains created by electronic communication and air travel. These gains, though helpful, nullify distances alive with romantic wonder and awe:

People [in the nineteenth century] knew less of each other, perhaps, but they felt more free of each other, and so were more individual. The entire world was not for them only a push or a switch away. Strangers were strange, and sometimes with an exciting, beautiful strangeness. It may be better for humanity that we should communicate more and more. But I am a heretic, I think our ancestors' isolation was like the greater space they enjoyed; it can only be envied. The world is only literally too much with us now.

The plot of *The French Lieutenant's Woman* turns on the Hardyesque motif of an undelivered message. Whereas Charles's tie with Sarah offers only disgrace, union with the Freeman dynasty promises money and power galore. Sam, guided by material self-interest, does not deliver Charles's letter to Sarah. But the undelivered letter casts no brooding shadow; no malignant fate beating down from Wessex grips Charles. That the letter never reaches Sarah is Charles's fault. Everything in Fowles's existential world is free, a potential vessel for human energy. The servant class, including Sarah, exerts great force on their elders and betters. Sam's betrayal both gives and takes away life. It puts Sarah out of Charles's grasp, probably forever, but it also gives Charles a mission. And the energy and endurance he pours into this mission strengthen him with a strength he had never known before. Sam's godlike influence continues even after he stops working for Charles. An anonymous note from Sam leads Charles to Sarah after Mary, significantly while pregnant, chances upon her in London.

III

Fowles uses contrast to knit the many strands of his book. An intricate weave of doubles or pairs—verbal, scenic, and dramatic—form the rigging of the contrast. The first of these doubles comes in the opening chapter—a frame that builds mood and setting as economically as the first chapters of *The Return of the Native, Nostromo,* or *A Passage to India.* The chapter plays Sarah, looking across Lyme Bay in her worn black coat, against the colorful, stylish couple, Ernestina and Charles. This arrangement foreshadows the last scene in the book, where Charles is by himself near another body of water, the Thames.

Some of Fowles's contrasts are playful: Charles kills a big slow bird called a *bustard,* but later evens the phonetic account by siring a bastard. Some are serious: trade, the bourgeois idol, smashes class barriers as neatly as sexual love, the great democratizer; hardly anybody in the book escapes the storekeeping syndrome. Charles is invited to work in Mr. Freeman's "yellow-tiered giant" on Oxford Street. His one-time servant, Sam, does take a job at Freeman's, and Sam's fortunes rise as steeply as Charles's drop. Money decides freedom, as well as personal identity, in Victorian England. Sam fulfills his vocational ambitions in direct ratio to his rising salary. Charles's link with a moneyless girl costs him his good name as well as the control of the Freeman millions.

Sometimes contrast balances the action of a chapter. In Chapter Nineteen, for instance, Sarah's chaste sleep with one of Mrs. Poulteney's maids balances the wideawake male union of Charles and Dr. Grogan under the banner of Darwinism. Chapter Twenty-one finds Mary and Sam confronting Sarah and Charles in the Undercliff. The chance confrontation is a mirror meeting: both couples are waging trysts; both are to move their base of operation from Lyme to London; both will produce offspring. A more extended looking-glass encounter comes when Charles goes to London to talk to Mr. Freeman. London, though more impersonal, reflects Lyme. Ernestina materializes in London as her father; Sarah Woodruff of

Lyme returns as ⟨Sarah Roughwood of London; Lyme's domestic tyrant, Mrs. Poulteney, balances Mr. Freeman, ruler of a commercial dynasty in London: a rich merchant like Mr. Freeman can balance two characters structurally in a novel set in a money-ruled (Agora) society) especially if the two characters are women. The love affair that hazard begins while Sarah is living with Mrs. Poulteney chills to formality in the office of Mr. Freeman's London attorney. In this scene, we also learn that Sarah's middle name and Ernestina's mother's first name are the same, that is, Emily. ⟨Sarah, finally, who worked as Mrs. Poulteney's companion-secretary, takes the same sort of job in London under another drug addict; while Mrs. Poulteney dosed herself nightly with laudanum, or opium, Dante Gabriel Rossetti died of chloral. The unlikely link between Mrs. Poulteney and Rossetti is forged by Sarah but also, more subtly, by Charles, who becomes "as dependent on traveling as an addict on his opium."

Chapter Thirty-eight takes Charles from the wood-paneled order of Mr. Freeman's Hyde Park study to the surreal night world of Mayfair. Each place is a battlefield; each leads to Freeman's on Oxford Street. To escape them, Charles goes, first, to a luxury brothel and, then, to the seedy flat of a street-walker named Sarah. Fowles's introduction of a second Sarah into the action works brilliantly. Just *how* brilliantly is borne out in an essay by Gilbert J. Rose, M.D. (Yale University School of Medicine, Department of Psychiatry). The essay, "Irredentism and the Creative Urge," stresses "the drive to reestablish unity with the lost mother of infancy" (p. 7). Dr. Rose grounds his thesis in the conflation of the novel's two ⟨Sarahs, noting that both Sarahs are abandoned by a soldier-lover and that both have a baby daughter. Then he joins the two years Charles's mother was married before she died bearing a daughter, the two years the Sarah of Chapters Forty and Forty-one has worked as a prostitute, and also the two years that pass between Charles's last two meetings with Sarah Woodruff.) Dr. Rose then argues (pp. 10-11) that Charles cannot establish a family at the end because his former sweetheart and daughter are "ghosts—revivified images" of his dead mother and sister, launched into fantasy-life by the nearby Thames, "image of the sea, that arch-symbol of birth" where the book started. The clash between fantasy and reality scatters grief all through Fowles. Charles's meetings in London with the two Sarahs both end in sexual setback. He does not sleep with the prostitute, and his visit to the Rossetti home does not win him a wife. Both Sarahs surprise Charles with baby daughters, whom he dandles and amuses with his watch. The ticking watch, Charles's instant liking for the two little girls, and the disappointment hedging both scenes all set his sexual failure within a frame of passing time and accumulated guilt welling up from the deaths of his mother and baby sister.

This guilt accounts for Charles's ineffectuality in general. It also underlies his openness to blackmail. In line with the book's mirrorlike form, Fowles presents the blackmail motif as a rhythmic pattern of repeated experience. Charles finds himself blackmailed sexually by Sarah, socially by Sam, and morally by both Mr. Freeman and Dr. Grogan. These threats recall Nicholas Urfe's practice of converting all events into aesthetic sensations. If all the world's a stage, then moral guilt is just a dramatic illusion. Urfe's practice of weaving fiction into his actions carries into *The French Lieutenant's Woman.* Alone in his room, Charles flings out his arms "as if to an audience, an actor accepting applause." One of Charles and Sarah's key meetings takes place in "a kind of minute green amphitheater." And in a scene that owes a debt to Thackeray's picture of himself as puppeteer at the end of *Vanity Fair*—another novel with more than one ending—Fowles enters the last chapter as a successful impresario. Elsewhere, characters act roles: Sam plays the meek footman for Charles's sake; Charles affects the dutiful nephew for his uncle; Ernestina is the biddable ingenue, Sarah the fallen woman, and Mrs. Poulteney the charitable Christian. In line with the Darwinian principle of cryptic coloration, role-acting helps these characters adapt to their surroundings. Yet Fowles takes it beyond Darwin. If evolution is to steer the future, it cannot rely on unconscious change alone. Change must come from impulse and desire. The role-playing characters in *The French Lieutenant's Woman* describe evolution as a product of the will. They do adapt to their surroundings, but only to reshape and perhaps struggle past them.

The novel's most vexing (and most delicious) evolutionary puzzle comes in its most controversial scene, at the end. *The French Lieutenant's Woman* ends first in Chapter Forty-four with Charles resigning himself to marry Ernestina and to forget Sarah. Fowles, backing away from the Victorian nostrum of duty, calls this outcome, "a little too sweet to satisfy people's ideas about reality."[20] The sugary domestic finale of Chapter Forty-four, if allowed to end the action, would have canceled some of the novel's best moments: Sarah and Charles do not become lovers until Chapter Forty-six; Charles gets dragged before Mr. Freeman's lawyers in Chapter Fifty-six; he sails to America in Chapter Fifty-nine. To leave out scenes like these would have dimmed the novel's brilliance. Yet, for all their surge, these scenes distract from the book's main purpose. Both *The Magus* and *The French Lieutenant's Woman* present family living as life's most basic reality, the goal of a long and painful initiation rite. But neither book describes it. The closest Fowles comes to portraying domestic life is in *The Collector*. The demented conditions depicted there, though, do not clarify the tensions of ordinary homelife. No Chekhov, Lawrence, or Updike, Fowles devotes but few of his narrative skills to domestic realism. It is as if marriage ends a character's fun and freedom and also strips him of the force needed to motorize a serious novel. The best parts of *The French Lieutenant's Woman* may well come after the book's first ending; but these chapters are where Charles is most footloose. If Fowles has an artistic shortcoming, it rises from not challenging his existentialism with the test of marriage and family. He no sooner readies Urfe and Charles for this test than he leaves them.

But is it fair to attack Fowles for not doing something he never intended? Can there be failure without attempt? Readers are less tolerant of lapses from the hand of a gifted and disciplined writer than they are of similar imperfections in a lesser author. Fowles's neglect of family life is a lapse. As exacting and exciting as *The French Lieutenant's Woman* is, a head-on confrontation with domestic realism would have given the book a balance and relevance it now lacks. This confrontation starts to build in Chapter Sixty, the novel's second ending, where Sarah agrees to marry Charles. Sarah, as has been said, emerges here with new strength, harmony, and beauty. Lending warmth to this radiance is Lalage, Charles and Sarah's daughter. Charles's discovery of Lalage goes to his heart, if only briefly. The most he had looked for in his meeting with Sarah was a wife. The reward of a family outstrips his hopes. Yet this family reunion does not end the book. Instead, Fowles adds a chapter where Sarah turns down Charles's offer of marriage. The book's last ending, though the starkest of the three, has the strongest historical and evolutionary thrust. Sarah's rejection of Charles rests on two Brechtian principles: first, that all of us decay and evolve simultaneously and, next, that this shuttling motion both retards and aids progress, justice, and the rule of love. The novel's third ending also shows, like Brecht's history plays, man's freedom to change over time. The changes that two years create in both Sarah and Charles express the changeability of the world.

Chase rhapsodizes over Sarah's growth: "Sarah Wood-ruff's transformation, the most significant single element in the book, is from total servitude and dependence to ultimate self-knowledge and mastery."[21] He is only partly right. What he has forgotten is the stiff resistance *all* change meets, both within and outside the individual. Sarah *has* carved out a challenging, exciting way of life. The Rossetti circle forms "a community of honorable endeavor, of noble purpose." Its fusion of poetry and painting extends artistic frontiers. It also creates a new personality for Sarah within the sphere of women's liberation, Victorian England's most crying social need. McDowell's statement on the novel's third ending sees her as an evolutionary force:

> In an age dominated by the dynamism of Darwin's ideas, Sarah might regard herself as a pioneer in the emancipation of her sex; refuse the fulfillments of love, marriage, and home; and work to bring about increased freedom in social usages and institutions.[22]

Sarah's changing her name from Woodruff to Roughwood, her hiring on again as an amanuensis, and her working for another drug addict denote the crabwise motion of evolution. Following the Darwinian principle of cryptic coloration, she has changed her colors and clothes to blend with her avant-garde surroundings. And in her bright new plumage she has thrived.

But she has thrived by joining the establishment of rebellion. Comfortable and socialized within her coterie, she takes no risks. Her colorful new self, though a great advance from her earlier drabness, is closed-ended. Sarah has shut out hazard. What she fears particularly is the toll that marrying Charles will have on her mystery. McDowell discusses her failure to integrate mystery with the daily limits and renewals of love:

Her new-found purpose might . . . end by constricting her
possibilities for development as a human being. In this view of
Sarah, Charles sees paradoxically that he is ultimately freer than
she is because he can spontaneously give more of himself than she
can. Her imagination out-runs passion . . . The irony is that she
outgrows, not altogether to her advantage as a person, the claims
of passion before Charles's inhibitions are overcome. Charles,
has, however, a truer intimation as to the process of evolution
than Sarah; it operates, he sees, with a side-wise and contingent
motion rather than with a clearly discerned forward one. [23]

Sarah's adaptation, then, leaves Charles at the novel's
thematic heart. The third ending of *The French Lieutenant's
Woman* neither ignores reality nor leaks into naked indeterminacy. Rather, it puts forth the key truths of Fowles's
vision—mystery, hazard, and freedom as a function of loss
and apartness. Charles stands in the last chapter where Sarah
stood in the first—alone. He belongs nowhere. But only the
outcast presses for change; socialized people like Sarah
Roughwood do not strain enough against their environment to
serve progress. Charles's freedom is cruel but necessary. Out
of his existential dread springs the hope of transcending
history. At the end, Charles is no longer comical, but brave.
He has cut loose from his age's pieties; his vision of union with
Sarah has cracked; he has neither friends nor a job. The
Victorians had many nostrums to hide behind, but he rejects
them all to struggle toward the new century. Just as Urfe be-
came an embryo sprite or magician (Ur-fay) at the end of *The
Magus,* Charles too joins in an elaborate birth that includes
Sarah, Lalage, and the coming century.

In a 1969 interview for *Time,* Fowles said, "The whole
human condition is slavery, and self-liberation is that little
flash in the darkness for the individual." [24] This summary of
Fowles's personalist ethic applies vividly to Charles. As has
been noted, Charles hammers life out of the smithy of his
crushed ego. The flash that pulses through him lifts him out of

the realm of melodrama and into that of tragedy. What will the flash kindle? How long and how brightly will it glow? These questions go beyond the purview of the novel. What is more immediate is that Charles makes us ask them. He has learned something, and Fowles respects him for it. His waiting, aimless wandering, and suffering make Charles's flash very expensive. But like the fortune in money, time, and effort that went into Urfe's apprenticeship, the flash is evolutionally cheap. What Urfe and Charles attain in a year or two must normally wait hundreds of thousands of years. Evolution is so slow because it spends centuries trying different possibilities before settling on the best one. People like Sarah, Charles, and Maurice Conchis sidestep this costly trial and error.

These characters introduce new forces into the push-pull drama of evolution. The loose-limbed freedom of the centuries-long drama makes room for the new force in the dialectic. Evolution depends on hazard. Uncaring and unconscious, it does not know if one of its parts has been preconditioned to speed its dumb, dragging tempo. What happens is this: evolution seizes the chance occurrence, tests it, integrates it, and then turns it into biological law. Bad luck, public indifference, and reversion to biological type will pad the jolt made by Charles and Urfe. But their sort will not vanish. Their followers will extend cultural frontiers; one or two like them in each generation will, after centuries, grow to hundreds. The Aristos will thrive.

Organism rather than machine, *The French Lieutenant's Woman* is like a great plant rooted in the past and branching into the future. This scope makes it Fowles's boldest and most inclusive work, proving his skill as storyteller, analyst, and diagnostician. The artistry and intellectual drive of *The French Lieutenant's Woman* claim our attention. Creatures in a contingent universe, we cannot afford to ignore the book's challenge.

NOTES TO CHAPTER 4

1. *See* Henry Chessell, *A Portrait of Lyme* (Bracknell, Berks.: Town and Country Press, 1969); Henry Chessell, *In Search of Lyme: A Street by Street Guide of Lyme* (Lyme Regis: Lyme Regis Printing Co., 1970); Ian Griffiths, *The Story of Old Lyme* (Lyme Regis: Lyme Regis Printing Co., n.d.).

2. E. Royston Pike, *Human Documents of the Victorian Golden Age (1850-1875)* (London: George Allen and Unwin, 1967), p. 8.

3. Fowles, "Notes . . . ," p. 161.

4. Oates, p. 3.

5. Edward T. Chase, "Delectable Novel," *New Republic*, 15 November 1969, p. 23.

6. Frederick P.W. McDowell, "Recent British Fiction: Some Established Writers," *Contemporary Literature* 11, no. 3 (Summer 1970): 430.

7. Ibid., p. 428.

8. Phyllis R. Katz, "The French Lieutenant's Woman," *Best Sellers*, 15 November 1969, p. 323.

9. Fowles, "Notes . . . ," p. 166.

10. McDowell, p. 428.

11. Ian Watt, "The French Lieutenant's Woman, New York *Times Book Review*, 9 November 1969, p. 74.

12. John Fowles, "Afterword," in Alain-Fournier, *The Wanderer*, or *The End of Youth*, trans., Lowell Bair (New York: Signet, 1971), p. 209.

13. Watt, p. 1.

14. Fowles, "Guide to a Man-Made Planet," p. 8.

15. John Fowles, "My Recollections of Kafka," *Mosaic* 3 (Summer 1970):37.

16. Geoffrey Grigson, *The Englishman's Flora* (London: Phoenix, 1955), p. 342.

17. Davenport, p. 1,225.

18. Oates, p. 1.

19. Fowles, "Weeds, Bugs, Americans," p. 99.

20. Stolley, p. 60.

21. Chase, p. 24.

22. McDowell, p. 429.

23. Ibid.

24. "Imminent Victorians," *Time*, 7 November 1969, p. 108.

Bibliography

BOOKS:

The Collector. London: Jonathan Cape; Boston: Little, Brown, 1963.

The Aristos: A Self-Portrait in Ideas. London: Jonathan Cape; Boston: Little, Brown, 1964. Revised ed., 1970.

The Magus. London: Jonathan Cape; Boston: Little, Brown, 1965.

The French Lieutenant's Woman. London: Jonathan Cape; Boston: Little, Brown, 1969.

Poems. New York: Ecco Press, 1973.

The Ebony Tower. London: Jonathan Cape; Boston: Little, Brown, 1974.

Shipwreck. London: Jonathan Cape, 1974; Boston: Little, Brown, 1975. Photography by the Gibsons of Scilly.

ARTICLES AND ESSAYS:

"On Being English and Not British." *Texas Quarterly* 7, no. 3 (Fall 1964): 154-62.

"On Writing a Novel." *Cornhill,* no. 1060 (Summer 1969), pp. 281-95. Reprinted as "Notes on an Unfinished Novel," in *Afterwords: Novelists on Their Novels,* edited by Thomas McCormack (New York and Evanston, Illinois: Harper & Row, 1969), pp. 160-75.

"My Recollections of Kafka." *Mosaic* 3, no. 4 (Summer 1970): 31-41.

"Jacqueline Kennedy Onassis and other First (and Last) Ladies."

Cosmopolitan, no. 170 (October 1970), pp. 144-49.

"Weeds, Bugs, Americans." *Sports Illustrated,* 21 December 1970, pp. 84-88, 90, 95-96, 99-100, 102.

"Making a Pitch for Cricket." *Sports Illustrated,* 21 May 1973, pp. 100-103.

AFTERWORD AND INTRODUCTIONS:

Afterword. In Alain-Fournier, *The Wanderer,* or *The End of Youth.* Translated by Lowell Bair. New York: Signet, 1971, pp. 298-23.

Introduction. Arthur Conan Doyle, *The Hound of the Baskervilles.* London: Jonathan Cape, 1974.

Introduction. Piers Brendon. *Hawker of Morwenstow.* London: Jonathan Cape, 1975.

INTERVIEWS:

Newquist, Roy, ed. "John Fowles." *Counterpoint.* New York: Simon & Schuster, 1964, pp. 217-25.

Sage, Lorna. "Profile 7: John Fowles." *The New Review* 1, no. 7 (October 1974): 31-37.

TRANSLATION:

Perrault, Charles. *Cinderella.* London: Jonathan Cape, 1974.

REVIEWS:

"The Most Secretive of Victorian Writers, a Kind of Giant Mouse." New York *Times Book Review,* 21 June 1970, p. 4. Review of J. Hillis Miller, *Thomas Hardy: Distance and Desire* (Harvard University Press).

"Guide to a Man-Made Planet." *Life,* 4 September 1970, pp. 8-9. Review of Angus Wilson, *The World of Charles Dickens* (Viking).

Review of Marshall McLuhen, with Wilfred Watson. *From Cliche to*

Archetype (Viking), *Saturday Review,* 21 November 1971, pp. 32-33.

"Outlook Unsettled." *New Statesman,* 26 January 1973, pp. 130-31. Review of Emmanuel Le Roy La Durie, *Times of Feast, Time of Famine,* translated by Barbara Bray (Allen and Unwin).

"Gory Details." *New Statesman,* 9 March 1973, pp. 345-46. Review of Earle Hackett, *Blood: The Paramount Humour* (Jonathan Cape).

"Country Matters." *New Statesman,* 27 April 1973, pp. 620-21. Review of Ian Newton, *Finches,* and Michael Proctor and Peter Yeo, *The Pollination of Flowers* (both Collins New Naturalist).

"Voices of the Deep." *New Statesman,* 15 June 1973, pp. 892-93. Review of D.E. Gaskin, *Whales, Dolphins, and Seals* (Heinemann), and Karl-Erik Fichtelius and Sverre Sjolander, *Man's Place,* translated by Thomas Teal (Gollancz).

"All Too Human." *New Statesman,* 20 July 1973, pp. 90-91. Review of M.R. Hays, *Birds, Beasts, and Men* (Dent).

"A Lost World." *New Statesman,* 3 August 1973, pp. 154-55. Review of Flora Thompson, *Lark Rise to Candleford* (Penguin).

"Other Edens." *New Statesman,* 12 October 1973, pp. 524-25. Review of Derek Pearsall and Elizabeth Salter, *Landscapes and Seasons of the Medieval World* (Elek).

"Late Harvest." *New Statesman,* 26 October 1973, pp. 612-13. Review of John Stewart Collis, *The Worm Forgives the Plow* (Charles Knight).

"Unnatural Habitats." *New Statesman,* 14 December 1973, p. 912; Review of Richard Mabey, *The Unofficial Countryside* (Collins), Michael Chinery, *Insects of Britain and Northern Europe* (Collins), and Alice M. Coats, *The Book of Flowers* (Phaidon).

"Menhirs Maketh Man." *New Statesman,* 22 March 1974, pp. 412-13. Review of Gerald S. Hawkins, *Beyond Stonehenge* (Hutchinson) and John Michell, *The Old Stones of Land's End* (Garnstone).

"Softer than Beef." *New Statesman,* 10 May 1974, pp. 664-65. Review of Piers Paul Read, *Alive* (Secker and Warburg).

"Bleeding Hearts." *New Statesman,* 14 June 1974, pp. 842-43. Review of Ronald Fletcher, *The Akenham Burial Case* (Wildwood House).

"Missing Beats." *New Statesman,* 13 September 1974, p. 352. Review of Marglad Evans, *Autobiography* (Calder and Boyars).

STUDIES OF JOHN FOWLES

Berets, Ralph. *"The Magus:* A Study in the Creation of a Personal Myth." *Twentieth-Century Literature* 19 (1973): 89-98.

Boston, Richard. "John Fowles, Alone but not Lonely." New York *Times Book Review* 9 November 1969, pp. 2, 52, 54.

Bradbury, Malcolm, "John Fowles's *The Magus."* In *Sense and Sensibility in Twentieth-century Writing.* Edited by Brom Weber. Carbondale and Edwardsville, Illinois: Southern Illinois University Press, 1970, pp. 26-38. Reprinted as "The Novelist as Impresario: John Fowles and His Magus." In *Possibilities: Essays on the State of the Novel.* London and Oxford: Oxford University Press, 1973, pp. 256-71.

Brantlinger, Patrick, Adam, Ian, and Rothblatt, Sheldon. *"The French Lieutenant's Woman:* A Discussion." *Victorian Studies* 15 (1972): 339-56.

Churchill, Thomas. "Waterhouse, Storey, and Fowles: Which Way Out of the Room?" *Critique* 10, no. 3 (1968): 72-87.

De Vitis, A.A. and Palmer, William J. *"A Pair of Blue Eyes Flash at The French Lieutenant's Woman. Contemporary Literature* 15, no. 1 (Winter 1974): 90-101.

Evarts, Prescott, Jr. "Fowles's *The French Lieutenant's Woman* as Tragedy." *Critique* 13, no. 3 (1971): 57-69.

Halpern, Daniel and Fowles, John. "A Sort of Exile in Lyme Regis." *London Magazine* 10 (March 1971): 34-46.

Hauptfuhrer, Fred. "His Stories Are Riddles Wrapped Inside an Enigma Named John Fowles." *People,* 7 April 1975, pp. 56-59.

Kane, Patricia. "The Fallen Woman as Free-Thinker in *The French Lieutenant's Woman* and *The Scarlet Letter." Notes on Contemporary Literature* 2, no. 1 (1972): 8-10.

Kaplan, Fred. "Victorian Modernists: Fowles and Nabokov." *Journal of Narrative Technique* 3 (1973): 108-20.

Laughlin, Rosemary M. "Faces of Power in the Novels of John

Fowles." *Critique* 13 no. 3 (1971): 71-88.

"No PLR Candidate for St. Marylebone." *Bookseller,* 17 October 1970, no. 3382, pp. 2098-99.

Palmer, William J. *The Fiction of John Fowles: Tradition, Art, and the Loneliness of Selfhood.* Columbia, Missouri: University of Missouri Press, 1974.

Rackham, Jeff. "John Fowles: The Existential Labyrinth." *Critique* 13, no. 3 (1971): 89-103.

Rose, Gilbert J. *"The French Lieutenant's Woman:* The Unconscious Significance of a Novel to Its Author." *American Imago* 29 (1972): 165-76.

Scholes, Robert. "The Orgiastic Fiction of John Fowles." *The Hollins Critic* 6, no. 5 (December 1969): 1-12.

Stolley, Richard B. "The French Lieutenant's Woman's Man." *Life,* 29 May 1970, pp. 55-60.

Tatham, Michael. "Two Novels: Notes on the Work of John Fowles." *New Blackfriars* 5 (September 1971): 404-11.

Rubenstein, Roberta. "Myth, Mystery, and Irony: John Fowles's *The Magus,"* *Contemporary Literature,* XVI (Summer 1975), 3: 328-339.

Errata for *John Fowles, Magus and Moralist*

Page 174—Rubenstein entry should precede Scholes entry.

Page 175, column 1, line 7—*Alexandria Quarter* should read *Alexandria Quartet*

Page 176, column 1, line 11—Falubert should read Flaubert.

Page 176, column 1, line 20—insert comma after feminism in.

Page 176, column 1, line 30—insert space after 43,; 45-57 should read 45-47.

Page 176, column 1, line 33—insert 35, after 33,.

Page 176, column 1, line 34—59 should read 49.

Page 177, column 1, line 10—insert comma after 129-31.

Page 177, column 2, line 19—insert comma after *Portrait.*

Index